# The Disconnect Principle

# THE DISCONNECT PRINCIPLE

# PRINCIPLE

Eliminate difficult conversations with clarity and empathy

ANN LATHAM

First published in 2022 by Intellectual Perspective Press

To find out more about our authors and books visit:
www.intellectualperspective.com

# CONTENTS

# PRAISE FOR THE DISCONNECT PRINCIPLE

The Disconnect Principle *bridges the gap in previous training I've received on feedback and coaching. Ann provides clear examples of how to improve both of these critical tasks every employee and manager have. These tips work in multiple aspects of our personal lives as well.* The Disconnect Principle *should be required reading for all people who lead/manage others.*

Mark Davis, Director Food Safety, PepsiCo

*At* The Business Influencer Magazine *we champion the dissemination of thought provoking ideas that can change the world and make us better human beings. Ann's latest book is one such offering. If you hate those miserable conversations about performance,* The Disconnect Principle *will make all the difference. It's another brilliant book from Ann Latham with the power to change how we think. Dare I say – it's as disruptive in nature as her last book,* The Power of Clarity.

Ninder Johal DL, publisher, *The Business Influencer Magazine*

*Ann Latham's* Disconnect Principle *will make one of a manager's toughest jobs — giving feedback — smoother and more rewarding. The mindset shift she recommends will take the sting out of difficult performance conversations and let you be the empathic, effective leader you aspire to be.*

Daniel H. Pink, #1 *New York Times* bestselling author of *The Power of Regret, Drive,* and *To Sell Is Human*

*Just when I thought Ann Latham couldn't demystify and simplify another critical leadership/management concept that vexes all of us, here comes* The Disconnect Principle. *Like* The Power of Clarity, *Ann's new book unlocks easy to implement frameworks.*

Dan Horowitz, Senior Director, LinkedIn

*We all know feedback is a necessary and important part of improving at work – but delivering it can be awkward for many managers.* The Disconnect Principle *will change how you manage employee performance forever, helping you lead with pragmatism and empathy.*

Dorie Clark, *Wall Street Journal* bestselling author of *The Long Game* and executive education faculty, Duke University Fuqua School of Business

The Disconnect Principle *is packed with engaging examples and practical advice to improve your team's dialogue today. Fantastic!*

Dr. Marshall Goldsmith is the *Thinkers50* #1 Executive Coach and *New York Times* bestselling author of *The Earned Life, Triggers,* and *What Got You Here Won't Get You There*

# SMACKED ... RIGHT BETWEEN THE EYES!

Max was a good leader, a smart and thoughtful man, and sincerely interested in improving his skills and strengthening his team. His company was successful and he was striving to capitalize on their success and learn from every shortcoming. His team appreciated his talents, and they all seemed to work pretty darn well together.

Until someone screwed up.

After that, no matter what approach Max took, things never turned out as he hoped. Sometimes he felt he was too soft, cushioning his comments so carefully that the importance of his message was lost. That made him feel weak and inept—qualities that didn't sit well with his image of himself or his ideas of good leadership.

Other times Max felt his approach was too strong. Too firm. His employee got defensive and upset. As he limped out of the room, his mind was furiously rationalizing, projecting blame, rewriting the conversation—anything to prevent himself from feeling like he was the one who just screwed up. Often, the relationship remained tense for weeks after these encounters, and yet the problem was not completely resolved. He felt unfair and mean. As a leader, he knew strength was important, but he certainly didn't want to be unfair or mean. That's not how he saw himself.

And then there were the times when Max just let it go. He couldn't face more drama, especially at that particular moment, especially with that particular employee. In those cases, he either convinced himself that it would be better to let this one incident slide or he just kept putting it off ... and putting it off ... until raising the issue made no sense. Or, until something similar happened again. And again. Max was not, by nature, a procrastinator. What was happening to him? He could see the damage this behavior caused, and yet he caught himself backing away when action was obviously needed. He struggled to walk into another difficult conversation that would leave him either wimping out or limping away with tail between his legs once again.

Finally, Max turned to me. "What am I doing wrong?"

I quickly taught him everything I knew about giving feedback. Then I prepped him for a particularly sensitive situation. We identified the situation, behavior, and impact. I made sure he was relying on facts and leaving out assumptions. I made sure he could describe the impact clearly and specifically. I helped him prepare, choose a good time and place, and determine the order he would use to open the meeting and address the issues. We discussed language. Words he should use. Words to avoid. Ways to phrase his concerns.

When Max walked into that meeting with his employee, he stood tall and confident. He was ready.

And then … he failed again.

When we debriefed later, he was in pain. Angry with his employee. But even angrier with himself. He was demoralized. His behavior did not reflect the positive, helpful man he wanted to be.

That's when I had my epiphany. That's when I recognized what was missing from the many best practices prescribed for delivering effective feedback. That's when I discovered the Disconnect Principle. And that's what I will teach you in this book.

There is nothing wrong with all the best practices you have learned. It is the omissions of those best practices—the advice they *didn't* include that is the key to clear, comfortable, empathic, and effective discussions about employee performance. The Disconnect Principle is the missing link.

Max is not the only leader I've seen struggle with feedback, accountability, and performance management. Between my own corporate career and then almost twenty years of consulting, I've known these struggles and seen these struggles in others.

I've felt and witnessed the discomfort, self-doubt, feelings of inadequacy, reluctance to address performance issues, and the almost-false personalities people adopt when trying to hold others accountable.

I'm all too familiar with the mismanaged problems that drag on, worsen, and suck the energy and optimism out of managers and coworkers.

I've seen the damage done to relationships as well.

All of these struggles occurred while good people carefully tried to apply everything they had been taught about setting expectations, giving feedback, and holding others accountable.

If you can't talk about employee performance clearly, comfortably, and empathically, how can you hope to manage others and ensure accountability?

When you read *The Disconnect Principle*, you will discover the critical ingredients for success that you've been missing. The principle I discovered watching Max suffer despite our careful preparation, *plus* everything I've learned since then about applying that principle. You will learn the secret to confident, timely action. You will understand how to eliminate those painful conversations in favor of clear, comfortable, pragmatic problem solving while growing strong, trusting relationships. Maybe best of all, you will learn how to be your authentic self and leave your boss face in the drawer. You will see that you can stop worrying about being unkind or unfair because you will be confident that your behavior demonstrates kindness, empathy, and *fairness*.

Once you embrace the Disconnect Principle, you won't have to steel yourself for those difficult conversations or prepare scripts or tiptoe around difficult coworkers. You won't be replaying conversations repeatedly in your mind, hoping that one more pass will make you feel better. You won't have to choreograph your movements to avoid running into someone before you are ready to "have that conversation." You won't have to play the terminator. And you won't fight the us vs. them battles since you will no longer be a "them" and everyone will have a greater sense of "us."

Setting expectations, feedback, accountability, and performance management collectively represent one of those perennial problems like unproductive meetings, cognitive uptimes maxing out at 20%, and insufficient clarity. Despite endless articles, courses, and advice, results are unchanged. Until now. *The Disconnect Principle* does for managing others what my previous book, *The Power of Clarity*, has done for the productivity and effectiveness of knowledge workers, managers, and executives. I hope you find it as powerful as my clients have.

Interested in harnessing the power of clarity?
Download the introduction to my book, *The Power of Clarity*, at DisconnectPrinciple.com

The Disconnect Principle offers a new approach. Let's say goodbye to difficult conversations and hello to clarity, empathy, and pragmatic action!

# 1.

# "WE HAVE A DISCONNECT!"

---

The Disconnect Principle is quite simple and goes like this:

*"When something doesn't go the way you expected, all you know for certain is that something didn't go the way you expected."*

You probably don't know what really did or didn't happen. You certainly don't know why. And if you make assumptions or leap to conclusions, you will likely be wrong, probably unfair, and almost certainly insulting.

Thus, when your expectations aren't met, the best response is clear: "*We have a disconnect.*"

When you say this, you put the focus on the situation, not the person.

Your goal is to fix the situation, not the person.

This approach ensures you treat people with respect and prepare yourself to listen and learn as you try to figure out:

- What needs to be done next and/or
- How to prevent a recurrence.

# You truly don't know what

The Disconnect Principle emphasizes how little we really know when our expectations aren't met. It takes us back to a point where we aren't even sure whose behavior may be involved. It takes us back to a point where blame isn't possible because all we know is that something didn't go as we had hoped. All we know for certain is that we have a "disconnect."

---

**The Disconnect Principle:**
When something doesn't go the way you expected, all you know for certain is that something didn't go the way you expected.

---

# You certainly don't know why

The potential reasons for something not happening as expected are extensive. Consider the following and all the variations on these themes limited only by your creativity:

- No one understood your expectations.
- The person you expected to do something didn't think it was their responsibility.
- That person misunderstood your expectations.
- That person knew it was their responsibility, but other priorities or obstacles prevented action.

- That person was stopped by fear to act or concerns about whether the action was a good idea.
- That person needed help and couldn't get it, was afraid to ask, or got help that was misguided.
- That person did what they thought was best, knowing it wasn't exactly what you wanted.

I could go on, but put yourself on the receiving end and you will come up with even more possibilities. None of these are screwups by anyone, except maybe you because you didn't make yourself clear or you made the request of the wrong person at the wrong time.

Thus, when something doesn't go as you expected, all you know for certain is that something didn't go as you expected and there was a disconnect!

## Why is the Disconnect Principle so powerful?

The beauty of the Disconnect Principle is the way it levels the playing field and forces everyone to step back and examine the facts without blame. It makes it so much easier to treat others with the respect they deserve. If you truly embrace this principle, you will not leap to blame or make assumptions. You will ask questions—honest, open questions. The only thing you will assume is that everyone was doing their best and acting with the best intentions. Now let's watch this play out.

Christy's new staff member wasn't quite measuring up. A client of mine believed that his team was bearing the brunt of the new employee's mistakes. He was concerned, both for his team and for the new employee. He wanted to be sure she got off to a good start in her new job.

While talking with my client, he told me that he was preparing to give Christy feedback about how she needed to do a better job of onboarding her new employee. I stopped him immediately to explain the Disconnect Principle. After listening carefully, my client realized that all he knew for sure was that the new employee was struggling to meet obligations. Somewhere, there was a disconnect!

He had no idea what Christy was or wasn't doing. He knew nothing about the employee's capabilities and challenges. He didn't know whether any other employees were involved. He didn't know if the employee was having trouble with other groups in addition to his own. He didn't know whether Christy even knew about the ways in which her new employee wasn't measuring up.

As a result of these realizations, he embraced the Disconnect Principle. Instead of worrying about how to approach Christy, he suddenly found it really easy. He mentioned that the employee seemed to be struggling, likely from a disconnect, and then waited to see Christy's reaction. He realized that she may have been spending a lot of time with this employee and going crazy over her slowness or inability to adjust. When my client didn't get that reaction, he simply told Christy that he wanted to be sure she knew that the employee hadn't come through on two recent commitments. Whether this surprised Christy or not didn't matter. He then offered his help. Christy was grateful and said she would think about it and let him know if she could use his help.

Imagine if, instead, my client had walked into Christy's office and even hinted that he didn't think she was managing her new employee well or that she needed to do a better job of onboarding her new employee. No matter what carefully chosen words he had used, no matter how much he planned the conversation, it would not have gone well because, in his mind, Christy was not doing her job well.

Christy was no dummy. She would have heard the assumption in his voice, if not in his words. She would have been angry if she had been devoting great effort to helping the new employee and she would have been embarrassed if not and caught by surprise. In either case, the conversation could easily have been extremely hurtful and unproductive, making my client miserable, ruining Christy's day as well, and possibly damaging their relationship for a long time to come.

The Disconnect Principle saved the day!

# Disconnects are ubiquitous!

When you proclaim "We have a disconnect," you are identifying a *really* common occurrence.

Before I go any further, let me emphasize that it's not just bosses whose expectations aren't met. Disconnects occur between coworkers, between teams, within teams, between collaborators, between employees and customers, and between employees and suppliers. Actually, they can occur between any two people anywhere. Period. And they can be flagged by either party, including from employee to boss. There is no one anywhere who hasn't experienced a disconnect and who wouldn't have benefitted from the simple, blame-free words that create an opportunity for regrouping and clarification. While many of the examples in this book are geared toward managers, everyone — and I mean everyone! — can use, "We have a disconnect." to signal a desire to sort things out without judgment.

> When your expectations aren't met, it doesn't matter whether you are dealing with a boss, a coworker, or a direct report. Your best response is, "We have a disconnect."

## Disconnects are ubiquitous

Expectations are easily established in our own minds, but not so easily transformed into results. Our thoughts and words embark on quite a journey when they leave our mouths.

The journey of a simple request

It's quite a journey, with so many potential disconnects! Actually, when you think about all of the potential disconnects in hearing, understanding, roles, method, priority, judgment, confidence, skill, execution, and communication, it's a wonder anything happens as you expect! It's like the game of telephone where a bunch of people sit in a circle and whisper a message from ear to ear until the originator gets to laugh at how far off the final message is from the original message.

# Investigating a disconnect

Once you recognize that you have a disconnect, it's time to investigate.

> "I was expecting you to _____. It seems something went awry because I don't think that's what happened."

Notice that the speaker here isn't even sure that the task wasn't completed! Maybe everything was done to perfection and she just missed the email notification! The next question is really easy: "Where are we on this?"

Then once you know where things stand, you can figure out how to get things rolling again. You clarify. You check for understanding, problems, conflicting priorities. You offer help. Your goal is success, not blame.

A "disconnect" is nonjudgmental. It levels the playing field, avoids blame, protects trust and respect, and puts problem solving front and center. It is simple and transformative.

But it isn't always easy. When I've taught the Disconnect

Principle to clients, they love it. They are really quick to latch onto the term. They start identifying and talking about disconnects instantly. Unfortunately, they often continue to struggle with resolving the disconnects. The fundamental problem is that many of our conventional management practices, beliefs, and habits prevent us from fully embracing and implementing the Disconnect Principle effectively. In further work with my clients, I identified those obstacles and that is why I have written this book.

Get your free poster, The Disconnect Principle – Pure and Simple, now at DisconnectPrinciple.com

So here is what you can expect for the rest of this book.

1. Appendix: I've put a short summary of the basics of giving feedback in the Appendix—the main best practices I taught Max before witnessing his failure and my subsequent epiphany. A quick scan of those practices by those of you who have had such training will ensure you know what I am talking about throughout the rest of the book. For those of you without that background, the Appendix will get you off to a good start and ensure my references make sense.

2. Chapters 2–6: These five chapters address each of the five obstacles I've uncovered since my epiphany—the

conventional thinking that prevents full adoption and successful application of the Disconnect Principle.

3. Chapter 7: *The mother of all disconnects*, addresses—you guessed it—the mother of all disconnects. Some of you will want to jump right there, which is fine, though there will be references to content from the intervening chapters. If you do jump, I hope you return to Chapters 2 through 6 later so you can truly embrace the Disconnect Principle and its incredible power.

4. Chapter 8: The final chapter, *Connecting through disconnects*, wraps up the many parts and paints a complete picture of the power of the Disconnect Principle.

I hope you enjoy the ride!

# Clear distinctions in summary

The Disconnect Principle is simple:

> *"When something doesn't go as you expected, all you know for certain is that something didn't go as you expected!"*

And the best response is, "We have a disconnect."

This simple statement puts all parties on equal footing with a shared goal to figure out where things stand, what to do next, and, in some cases, how to prevent a recurrence. There is no blame because no one is certain what actually transpired to cause the disconnect.

Learn how to embrace this principle so you can enjoy the following transformations (the rest of the book will tell you how):

| The old way | | With the Disconnect Principle |
|---|---|---|
| "You/they screwed up." | → | "That didn't turn out as I expected." |
| Perpetual frustration | → | Clarity, empathy, and pragmatic solutions |
| Difficult conversations | → | "We have a disconnect." |
| Fixing the person | → | Fixing the situation |

# 2.

# MIND CONTROL ... YOUR FIRST CHALLENGE

The way we think about feedback, accountability, and performance management prevents us from being the kind of human beings we want to be.

If you take a good look at all of the best practices for giving feedback mentioned in the Appendix and on the Internet, you will notice that they are all rules, tools, words, and tips for what you should *do*. While they provide good advice along those lines, they totally overlook what you should *think*. And the way we generally think about feedback, accountability, and performance management prevents us both from being clear, empathic, and effective and from feeling fair, helpful, reasonable, and confident.

This omission hit me square in the face when Max told me about his failed feedback conversation. Max *did* all the right things. But he lost the battle before he opened his mouth because he walked into that room thinking something like, "He screwed up again and I need to set him straight once and for all."

> The way we traditionally think about feedback,
> accountability, and performance management
> prevents us from being the kind of human beings we
> want to be.

While his words focused on the specific situation, observable behavior, and tangible impact of the employee's recent failure to meet expectations, Max was undoubtedly making a yeoman's effort to ignore past transgressions. In his mind, despite his prepared meeting format, he was inevitably dying to mention previous incidents that he had never properly conveyed or had failed to raise altogether. In his mind, he was reviewing past conversations that had accomplished nothing. Here he was again, trying to be nice when he was actually madder than hops. Max was way past the one simple situation in search of an improvement. He knew he was in the right; his employee was in the wrong. He had already decided that the employee needed to make major changes or he was out the door. That's all there was to it.

With those thoughts in his head, do you think Max was able to keep all of his strongly held conclusions out of his body language, tone of voice, gestures, and facial expressions?

And once Max's script ended and his employee reacted

defensively or aggressively, do you think Max's impromptu comments were empathic and judgment free?

And where would you put the odds that he was able to enter into a sincere problem-solving session where he listened with an open mind and gave his employee an honest opportunity to explain his side of the story?

Now consider the employee's side of this conversation. Do you think any employee would feel trusted and respected? Do you think they would be willing to share their thoughts openly and honestly? Is there any chance the employee is thinking this meeting is a constructive, mutually respectful problem-solving session?

> No matter how carefully you script your language, your thoughts will betray you. Your body language, tone of voice, and any impromptu words will make your true thoughts obvious to your employee.

If you think the odds of a happy, calm, and constructive conversation are greater than zero, you are an incurable optimist. This is not a recipe for success.

Max lost before he started. It's really not his fault, and, if you've been in this situation, it's really not your fault either because the advice you have received in the past only told you what to *do*, not what to *think*! That's a glaring omission. But here is the deal. You can't walk into these discussions with any thoughts akin to those lodged in Max's head. No matter how carefully you script your language, your thoughts will betray you. Your body language, tone of voice, and any impromptu words will make your judgmental thoughts obvious to your employee.

## The three components of feedback aren't what you expect

Let's start with the simple act of providing feedback.

When giving feedback, the process has three components. The first only involves taking care of your thoughts. Before you even think about meeting with someone to give feedback or discuss a performance concern, you must examine your thoughts. This is the step no one talks about.

**COMPONENTS OF
FEEDBACK**

A. YOUR THOUGHTS

↓

B. YOUR DESCRIPTION OF
BEHAVIOR AND IMPACT

↓

C. YOUR OFFER

The three components of giving feedback

Interestingly enough, skipping this first step is really common, and, if you have read my book *The Power of Clarity*, you know how often we skip first steps—and even second steps! And you know how unfortunate the consequences of these omissions can be! Well, in this case the consequences are equally dire!

Curious about *The Power of Clarity*? Download the introduction now at DisconnectPrinciple.com

The reason it is so important to take care of your thoughts should be pretty clear by now given what happened to Max. If you even thin thoughts like the following before giving feedback, you have already lost!

- I'm going to hold their feet to the fire.

- It's time to set them straight.
- They can't get away with this.
- I'm in the right, they're in the wrong.
- I've had about enough of this!
- They need to toe the line like everyone else.
- If this doesn't work, ....

Can you recognize yourself in any of those?

If not, perhaps your judgmental thoughts have been a bit milder:

- I'm going to fix them.
- They need constructive feedback.
- I'll rein them in, nicely, of course.
- They screwed up.

Any thoughts about controlling or correcting someone are unproductive. The Disconnect Principle is the best and most powerful way to take care of those thoughts. When your expectations aren't met and your response is, "We have a disconnect," you are stepping back and acknowledging how little you know. You deliver a nonjudgmental signal that it's time to listen and learn from each other so you can determine what did and didn't happen, what needs to be done next, and how to prevent a recurrence. When dealing with others and unmet expectations, you must take care of your mindset and dismiss any assumptions and judgments. Only then can you focus fairly, honestly, and objectively on the specific situation and the observable behavior and its impact. This is essential. Your goal has to be to fix the situation, not the person. And you can't do that if you are preoccupied with conclusions that judge the other person.

> The Disconnect Principle puts the focus on the *situation*, not a *person*. Your goal is to fix the *situation*, not a *person*.

# Clear distinctions in summary

The difference between what you've been doing that hasn't worked smoothly and success isn't the technique. It is the mindset. When you think in terms of disconnects, your words will reflect the Disconnect Principle and the mindset it fosters. The dynamic changes dramatically:

| The old way | | With the Disconnect Principle |
| --- | --- | --- |
| Relying on rules, tools, scripts, and tips to speak your mind | → | Taking care of your thoughts and seeking the disconnect |
| Knowing they screwed up again | → | Shedding preconceived notions |
| Adding this latest transgression to the case against the employee | → | Isolating and narrowing the focus to specific facts |
| Planning how to set them straight or rein them in | → | Recognizing how little you actually know about the situation |
| Scripting difficult conversations | → | Opening your mind to learning and unseen complications |
| Revealing your true thoughts with your body language, tone of voice, and impromptu words | → | Treating others with empathy respect and assuming good intentions |
| Feeling miserable and knowing your employee is just as mad or miserable | → | Working together comfortably to resolve issues |

The importance of our thoughts when entering into these conversations was my original epiphany after hearing about Max's botched conversation. Since then, I have recognized several additional impediments to making the Disconnect Principle work for my clients. The subsequent chapters address each of those factors one at a time.

3.

# ALL FEEDBACK IS CONSTRUCTIVE FEEDBACK

---

I remember the supervisory class I took early on that was most devoted to giving feedback. That was the first time I'd ever been told that the opposite of positive is not negative, but constructive!

However, all feedback *better* be constructive, because that's the point. The point is to be more effective. To do more of some things and less of others. To learn!

When you mince words or adopt euphemisms, you aren't clear. By talking about positive feedback, constructive feedback, or corrective feedback and actively avoiding the term negative feedback, you erode trust, confuse people, oversimplify the issues, and are less effective at helping others improve their performance. Worst of all, you enter a counterproductive mindset.

We work so hard to master difficult conversations when, truth be told, we could just as easily eliminate them with the Disconnect Principle. The previous chapter admonished you to take care of your thoughts. Now it is time to take that one step further and change the way we think about types of feedback. More specifically, we need to abandon the constructive feedback myth as it stands today so we can stop thinking in terms of correcting others.

# Word games erode sincerity and trust

I don't know who it was that thought it would be best to use the term constructive feedback, but I do know people aren't that stupid. Everyone knows the opposite of positive is negative. I didn't need my degree in mathematics to learn that lesson.

When you start talking about positive and constructive feedback, you are just playing word games. In this era, I am pretty sure you want to be seen as fair and authentic. I'm pretty sure you are a kind person who knows that trust and respect are the foundation of good relationships, both business and personal. If you want to preserve or build trust and respect, don't play word games. The term "constructive feedback" is just as awful as "right-sizing."

But don't worry, I don't want you to talk about positive and negative feedback either!

# Constructive AND positive

We got into trouble before anyone decided positive and constructive were opposites. The problem is the whole positive versus negative dichotomy when applied to feedback, impact, and employees. Good vs. evil. Cops and robbers. These models are too simplistic for human behavior and too judgmental. There are too many cops who do bad things and villains who do good things. We are complicated. How we choose to do what we do is complicated. And the consequences of what we do are usually equally complicated. Even very simple actions can result in some benefits and some unfortunate consequences.

Suppose your coworker, the show-off "genius," points out a mistake you made and you feel embarrassed. It's *good* that she noticed the mistake. We *want* people to notice mistakes. She should be *encouraged* to point out mistakes. Yet, it is unfortunate that you felt embarrassed. You should probably just get over it.

Now suppose this resident genius has a track record for pointing out mistakes and her coworkers frequently feel embarrassed or undermined. Maybe she does it in front of others. Maybe people don't want to work with her. Should they all just get over it? Or is it time to give the genius some "constructive feedback"?

This situation has the potential of becoming a disaster. Once the genius develops a track record for pointing out mistakes and upsetting multiple people, she can easily be labeled a problem. A manager intervenes. Delivers constructive feedback. Concentrates on changing the genius's behavior. Next thing we know, the genius stops pointing out mistakes. Her coworkers are happy, but still making mistakes. The genius isn't happy. Neither are the customers as the mistakes go out the door. The genius will probably leave. No one learned anything. Not even the manager.

Even this simple example demonstrates the complexity of our behavior and its impact. The whole fiasco started when the genius's track record of upsetting coworkers merged with all the training we've had about bad behavior and constructive feedback. Look how quickly we fall into the trap we've set for ourselves with this simplistic model.

Here we have an employee who is doing a *great* thing by catching lots of mistakes. We *want* the genius to continue to find mistakes. We *want* her to continue to have the courage to speak up. We *might* also want her to change the way she points them out. AND we would *love* it if she could teach her coworkers how she finds those mistakes. Considering what is best for the company, the genius represents far more good than bad, but she has a negative reputation because of her track record of upsetting coworkers.

Meanwhile, we would rather her coworkers *applaud* and *thank* this quick, observant peer for finding their mistakes. We want them to be *grateful* for her skills. We also want them to either get over their embarrassment or be frank with their genius and tell her how she might soften the blow. AND we would *love* it if they would ask their dear genius to share her techniques or viewpoint so they can learn how to find their own mistakes. Considering what is best for the company, these coworkers actually ought to be the ones with the more negative image, not the genius.

"The annoying coworker" is a common situation that is only made worse by thinking in terms of positive and constructive behavior and feedback. When the genius was given "constructive" feedback, it was destructive. And I wouldn't be surprised if the manager, tired of all the complaints, forgot to include all of the positive feedback: her ability to find mistakes and her willingness to speak up. When we separate the positive from the negative, the very act of making the separation is harmful and leads to simplistic thinking. The negative acquires obvious urgency—the problem that needs solving—while the positive gets a hand wave, if not forgotten altogether.

We need to shed this whole positive/constructive mindset. It is too simplistic and leads us to putting employees in good and bad boxes. We are complicated. Our specific, observable behavior may be simple, but its impact can still be complicated. Not all good. Not all bad. We need to shed the positive/constructive, positive/ negative dichotomy and recognize that ALL feedback is constructive. But since "constructive" feedback is tainted with negativity, let's just call it feedback.

> All feedback is constructive AND positive because that's how we learn!

So now let's apply the Disconnect Principle to this situation involving the genius and her coworkers. Imagine if the first upset coworker had said, "We have a disconnect"—a clear, totally civil, nonjudgmental signal that something didn't go as expected. "When you pointed out my mistake in front of everyone during our meeting this morning, I was really embarrassed."

And then, imagine if the genius had said, "Oh, I'm sorry. I didn't mean to embarrass you, but I didn't think it would have been good for everyone in the meeting to proceed without knowing that some of the information was wrong." End of subject? Possibly.

Or maybe the genius added, "Do you have a suggestion for what I might have done differently?"

Your guess is as good as mine as to what might have transpired next. One possibility is that the coworker would have shrugged, would not have had any ideas to help the genius, and would have realized the onus was on her, not the genius. No drama. Just an employee disappointed in herself.

Or maybe the coworker would have had an idea. Maybe

she would have asked the genius if she would be willing to take a look at the next report *before* the meeting so that any mistakes could be corrected ahead of time.

Notice that this approach requires no conscious positive or constructive feedback. Furthermore, it is:

- Matter-of-fact
- Nonjudgmental
- Immediate
- And requires no escalation to higher levels of authority.

When we think in terms of positive and negative/ constructive feedback, it's a slippery slope to thinking in terms of good and bad employees. Let's avoid that completely, stop using the terms positive and constructive feedback, and take a simpler and richer approach to how we learn and improve performance.

> Throughout this book, many of my most important comments are highlighted in breakout boxes. If you would like see all of them in one place, go to DisconnectPrinciple.com and download The Quotable Disconnect Principle.

# Don't forget the point of feedback: better results

Our behavior is driven by our beliefs, knowledge, confidence, skill, habits, context, experience, and attitude, to name a few of the complexities behind what we do. No matter what we do, our behavior has an impact. We might see it, hear it, feel it, measure it, or ... read about it in the newspaper. With that feedback, we have an opportunity to learn. Those lessons affect our beliefs, knowledge, confidence, skill, habits, context, experience, and attitude. The more carefully we pay attention and develop our self-awareness, the more likely we are to adjust our behavior next time around.

Unfortunately, there are times when none of the above occur. When we don't see, hear, or feel the consequences of our behavior. Times when there is no automatic clear feedback, such as falling off a bike. When a coworker doesn't claim a disconnect, but goes away mad without comment. When a customer silently disappears without notice. When we have a manager who never helps us understand where we are excelling and where we have fallen short. Simply put, without feedback, we cannot learn what to do differently.

Then there are other times when we do see and hear something, but we aren't able to interpret what it means clearly. Maybe the genius saw that her coworker was upset, but figured she was just upset with herself for making the mistake (not an unreasonable conclusion). We know something broke, but not the cost or ramifications. We are pretty sure a customer wasn't happy with our answer, but don't know whether we had any other option, don't know the importance of the customer, don't know if it made any difference in the long run. Without help interpreting the implications of our behavior, we can struggle to draw appropriate conclusions and may conclude the exact opposite of what we should.

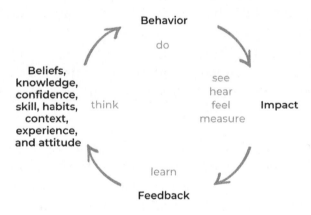

The performance circle

So, in addition to dismissing the good/bad dichotomy, remember that our goal is to improve performance. Not to label people or behavior as either good or bad, but to help people to do better by helping them see and/or interpret the impact of their actions so they know what to change and what to do more or less.

# Get the first component of feedback wrong and you will fail

The minute we think in terms of correcting others, we are off on the wrong foot with potentially disastrous consequences. The "You screwed up" mentality needs to be replaced with "We have a disconnect."

| INEFFECTIVE THINKING | COMPONENTS OF FEEDBACK | EFFECTIVE THINKING |
|---|---|---|
| Corrective | A. YOUR THOUGHTS | "We have a disconnect!" |
| | B. YOUR DESCRIPTION OF BEHAVIOR AND IMPACT | |
| | C. YOUR OFFER | |

You can lose before you begin if you don't take care of your thoughts!

# Clear distinctions in summary

Instead of mastering the art of difficult conversations, let's eliminate them with the Disconnect Principle. Take care of your thoughts. Avoid thinking in terms of correcting others by abandoning the constructive feedback myth. Instead, shift your thinking as follows:

| The old way | | With the Disconnect Principle |
|---|---|---|
| Some feedback is positive and other feedback is constructive | → | All feedback is constructive |
| Constructive is negative but we shouldn't call it that | → | Thinking positive vs. negative is destructive |
| The impact of behavior is either positive or negative | → | Impact is usually both |
| We have to deal with bad behavior | → | Behavior is intentional and unintentional with fortunate and unfortunate consequences |
| I need to give constructive feedback | → | "We have a disconnect." |

4.

# FIX THE SITUATION, NOT THE PERSON

---

We are quick to make quick assumptions about other people.

The problem is, most of those assumptions are destructive, if not completely false.

Furthermore, our judgment of others clouds the issue and prevents us from seeing the simple disconnects. It prevents us from figuring out what actually occurred. It prevents us from engaging with empathy, fairness, kindness, and respect. It prevents us from focusing on the disconnect instead of the person. It prevents us from being sure we are trying to fix the situation, *not* the person.

When working with clients, I frequently hear them describe their peers and direct reports as smart, ambitious, and knowledgeable. I also hear them talk about employees who are clueless, unambitious, lazy, and self-centered. The list of adjectives commonly used to describe others is pretty extensive. Some are clearly favorable traits and others obviously aren't.

This was also true when I was an employee. There was no shortage of descriptors used to describe others. Does this match your experience? What do you hear your coworkers say about others? What do you say about others?

Regardless of whether the adjectives are positive or negative, what they all have in common is that they are all spoken with conviction. Certainty. Complete confidence. We know laziness when we see it. We know ruthless ambition when it rears its ugly face. We recognize brilliance when we encounter it. We value those who are motivated, believe in our vision, and want to succeed.

## You can't see laziness

But there is a problem here. A big problem. And it interferes with our ability to use the Disconnect Principle to its full potential.

Why are we so certain about things we can't see?

skill
attitude
knowledge
experience
motivation
intentions
ambition
desires

These are all
**INVISIBLE!**

Why are we so certain about things we can't see?

You can't see laziness. You can't see ambition. Or knowledge. You can't see them because personal characteristics—attitudes, intentions, motivation, knowledge, desires, experience, and ambition—are all invisible. No one can see them. Which means no one can really know about them.

When Nancy is late three days in a row, we are quick to label her irresponsible. But she may just be having car trouble.

When Jordan is writing during a meeting, we might assume he is diligent in his note-taking. But he may be doodling or making a shopping list.

When Taylor fails to say good morning, thank you, and make small talk, we label her rude. But she may be super shy, super introverted, culturally disconnected, really busy, or just hard of hearing. I didn't greet classmates by name in high school, which likely made them think I was aloof, rude, or unfriendly, because I wasn't sure of their names! I had uncorrected near-sightedness coupled with a good dose of face-blindness. I was rarely certain who was walking toward me. It was safer for me to skip using names, a habit that continues to this day.

When Steve fails to object to a proposal, we assume he is in agreement with us. We assume he thinks the way we do (smart guy!) and will be committed to the project. But he may simply have given up. His objections have never mattered in the past, why object now? Why even pay attention?

Even skill is invisible. I remember the first night I ever waited tables. Unbeknownst to me, the experienced wait staff planned my initiation by assigning me to a large party headed by the owner of the resort who had a reputation for being grumpy and demanding and whom I hadn't met. When the meal was over, Papa John asked me where I had worked previously and who had trained me so well. He saw skill where there was only determination and hyper-vigilance.

Why do we make these assumptions? Why do we talk incessantly about characteristics we can't see? And why are we so certain in our assumptions?

# We are wired to make assumptions ... And they are usually wrong

Since we make so many assumptions, I can only conclude that we are wired to make assumptions. I'm sure this ability to make quick judgments has served our species well: knowing when to flee and when to fight. But in our modern lives, especially in our offices, homes, and communities, these judgments are far more likely to do harm than good.

First of all, we are likely to be wrong. Very likely. Think about the times you thought you screwed up and wanted to make amends with a friend or partner only to discover something completely different was the source of their stress. Your sense of guilt made you blind to other possibilities.

Think about the times you assumed someone was honest and truthful only to be badly burned.

Think about simple examples such as those above involving irresponsible Nancy, diligent Jordan, rude Taylor, and committed Steve.

Think also about Papa John and my "well-honed" table-waiting skills.

Truth be told, our assumptions about others are wrong

much of the time. And when our assumptions are wrong, it can be very destructive.

We might jump on Nancy for being irresponsible and warn her against being late again when what she really needs is help solving her car problems and, perhaps, a little sympathy. Imagine the damage to your relationship with Nancy and your own self-esteem if you fail to be supportive and adopt your tough love boss persona instead.

We might scorn Taylor for being rude before we learn the first thing about her. What are the chances of developing a strong relationship from such an inauspicious start?

We might praise Jordan for his diligent note-taking, which simply convinces him that it sure is easy to pull the wool over our eyes! He just found a brilliant way of dealing with our boring meetings!

# Name-calling is bad ... But you know that already

The greatest harm comes when the labeled person hears those assumptions about themselves. Whether the label is leveled directly or overheard, the damage is done. Think about how you feel when you are labeled. Think about how it feels to have any of those unkind adjectives pinned to you. Lazy, irresponsible, unreliable, clueless, weak, indecisive. We get angry, defensive, and vengeful. With good reason, I might add! We stop listening and focus on our comeback instead of anything else someone might be saying. No matter what words follow that label, communication is broken. The opportunity for a healthy, helpful conversation is past.

But you know that. And I hope you have enough control over your tongue to prevent the use of such labels.

What you might not realize is that characteristics that are usually considered positive can also feel negative: ambition, passion, and drive. If someone calls you ambitious, you might wonder whether what they are really saying is that you are too aggressive or ruthless. If someone calls you passionate, you might suspect what they really mean is that you are obsessed. Or if you are a woman, you might think they are accusing you of being too emotional.

Even accurate, agreeable characteristics can be problematic. You may relish being called meticulous today, but find it demeaning once promoted to a more strategic role. My mother was always sorting her children with labels and drawing conclusions about what we did and liked. She constantly put us in boxes, I guess in an effort to understand us. I hated it. Not only did it feel limiting and simplistic, but it didn't allow me to grow and change. At least not in her eyes. And when I did change, she drew attention to it, undue attention to things that didn't deserve attention, which was almost embarrassing.

Long story short, labels are name calling. We were taught

not to call people names in the playground as a child, but for some strange reason, it seems to be practiced regularly in the workplace and our everyday lives. Name-calling is hurtful, and even thinking of labels can eliminate the chance of a rational, problem-solving conversation that doesn't lead to defensiveness and a sudden loss of hearing.

# Ignore the invisible – even when it is hard

The Disconnect Principle and the feedback formula urge you to focus on observable behavior and its impact. When you say "We have a disconnect!," you are stepping back to examine the situation. This should keep you out of name-calling and labeling trouble, but it isn't easy because we are so quick to make assumptions. Pure and simple, it is a bad habit we don't always recognize. Thus, it all starts with awareness.

Which of the following are observable:

1. Bill was rude to his coworkers.
2. John doesn't care about others.
3. Kate acted pleased with her team.
4. Peg wasted a lot of time this afternoon.
5. Steve has poor judgment.
6. Lori is too ambitious and power-hungry.
7. Jim leaned forward, frowned and bit his lip while I spoke, and spoke when I stopped.

If you chose #7 and only #7, you are correct. The others are all assumptions.

> If you didn't choose #7 and only #7 or you know people who could benefit from this distinction between what's visible and what's not, go to DisconnectPrinciple.com and download the Visible vs. Invisible Workbook.

The first step toward change is understanding the current reality and its shortcomings. Thus, it is imperative that we realize how often we talk about invisible characteristics and make assumptions about others; both of which affect the way we behave toward others. Only then will it become easier to focus on observable behavior and its impact instead of personal characteristics. And doing so is a prerequisite for embracing the Disconnect Principle.

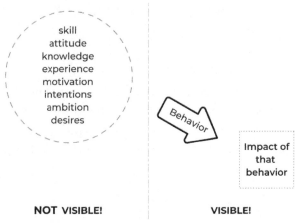

NOT VISIBLE! | VISIBLE!

Ignore the invisible; focus on the visible!

The Disconnect Principle states that when something doesn't occur as you expected, all you know for certain is that something didn't occur as you expected. From that conclusion, it is possible to investigate where things went astray so you can avoid the disappointment next time. It also allows you to figure out what did happen, specifically and clearly, so you can identify next steps and correct any unforeseen consequences. In both instances, the Disconnect Principle provides you the foundation you need to be clear, fair, empathic, and respectful while you sort out the disconnect. It will put the focus on the situation, *not* the person. Remember, your goal is to fix the situation, *not* the person!

We can't see 'lazy.'
We can't see 'unreliable.'
We can't see 'ambitious.'
Those are assumptions about invisible personal attributes.
When we make them, we damage our ability to treat people fairly and with an open mind.

The minute you allow yourself to make assumptions about others, about their personal characteristics that you can't see and can never know for certain, you erode your ability to treat missed expectations as a disconnect and your subsequent ability to be fair, empathic, and respectful.

# Never ever say never (or always)!

Another problem is generalizations. We all do it. Just the other day, the words "You never ..." came out of my mouth when talking with my husband. We both recognized it immediately. I stopped and made the correction before I got any further. Thank goodness! Because he was ready to be insulted!

The feedback formula admonishes us to be specific. There is nothing specific about "always" or "never." Furthermore, these generalizations are as false as our assumptions about others. Even someone who *never* does something probably has! At one time or another. Unless you watch someone twenty-four hours a day for life, you can never say never or always!

# Mastering the second component of feedback

| INEFFECTIVE THINKING | COMPONENTS OF FEEDBACK | EFFECTIVE THINKING |
|---|---|---|
| Corrective | A. YOUR THOUGHTS | "We have a disconnect!" |
| General, broad, include character assumptions | B. YOUR DESCRIPTION OF BEHAVIOR AND IMPACT | Specific, observable, focused on behavior and impact |
| | C. YOUR OFFER | |

Assumptions and generalizations can defeat you

The second component of feedback involves identifying the specifics of a situation. When you focus on the situation and not the person, generalizations, broad statements, and assumptions about personal characteristics are irrelevant and will ruin your chances of being effective. You must be specific and focus on visible behavior and its impact while purging all preconceived notions. "We have a disconnect!" will help avoid these common pitfalls.

> Fix the situation, *not* the person.

# Clear distinctions in summary

We are wired to make quick assumptions about the kind of people with whom we are dealing, but that tendency is not helpful in the workplace, and it's simply a bad habit. We can never really be certain of a person's invisible characteristics, so making assumptions about them, talking about them, and labeling them is only destructive.

Most important of all, our judgment of others clouds the issue and prevents us from seeing the simple disconnects. It prevents us from figuring out, with clarity and specificity, what actually occurred. It prevents us from engaging with fairness, kindness, and respect. It prevents us from focusing on the disconnect instead of the person.

Learn to ignore those invisible characteristics and you will shift your behavior as follows:

| The old way | | With the Disconnect Principle |
| --- | --- | --- |
| Frequent assumptions about invisible characteristics | → | Realizing how often we do it |
| "They are lazy / ambitious." | → | No more talk about what people are or aren't |
| Vague generalizations | → | A focus on clear, specific facts |
| Anger and frustration | → | Empathy and pragmatism |
| "They always screw that up." | → | "We have a disconnect." |
| "How can I fix them?" | → | "How can we fix this situation?" |

5.

# DO WITH, NOT TO

---

Back in my college days, I picked up the book *The Only Dance There Is* by Ram Dass. I am pretty quick to forget book titles and authors, so it is amazing that I still remember both from so many years ago. What is even more incredible is that I only read a tiny part of the book. And yet, the lesson I learned has stuck with me to this day. I can't quote him, of course. All I can do is tell you what I learned:

> When you try to do something TO someone, you usually fail. When you try to do something WITH someone, you are far more likely to succeed.

I suspect this rings true with you. When someone tries to control us, manipulate us, pressure us, or just tell us what to do, they are clearly trying to do something TO us, and we rarely respond well. It hurts our pride, crowds us, and takes away our sense of autonomy. Our reactions can range from visible or audible anger to quiet resentment and anxiety.

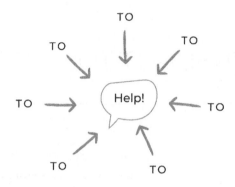

Doing TO

On the flip side, when someone is helpful and empathic, when they are clearly on our side and working WITH us, we feel supported and valued. Depending on the situation, we may also feel tremendous pride. Our sense of being in control and able to take responsibility is retained, if not greatly enhanced.

"Good ideas!"

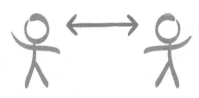

Doing WITH

# The third component of feedback

The third component of feedback is your offer to help resolve a disconnect or solve a problem. But how you try to help can make all the difference in the world.

The problem is that many of our default interactions with employees are examples of doing TO, not WITH. Hang on to your hat, because these may surprise you.

| INEFFECTIVE THINKING | COMPONENTS OF FEEDBACK | EFFECTIVE THINKING |
|---|---|---|
| Corrective | A. YOUR THOUGHTS | "We have a disconnect!" |
| General, broad, include character assumptions | B. YOUR DESCRIPTION OF BEHAVIOR AND IMPACT | Specific, observable, focused on behavior and impact |
| Doing TO | C. YOUR OFFER | Doing WITH |

The Disconnect Principle mindset

This diagram illustrating effective and ineffective thinking is available for download at DisconnectPrinciple.com. Look for Disconnect Principle Effective Thinking Diagram.

## Classic TO activities

Setting expectations can easily be a full out doing TO activity. When *you* set expectations by telling an employee exactly what *you* expect them to do, that's a TO.

Advising is also a TO. "You should do it this way." "You should think about X." "Please consider Y." (Should, should, should—I hate that word even when I apply it to myself!)

> When someone tries to control us, manipulate us, pressure us, or just tell us what to do, they are clearly trying to do something TO us, and we rarely respond well.

Teaching is another activity that is done TO others. Just picture all those reluctant students in classrooms around the world and you will know exactly what I mean. They are definitely being done TO. What does that have to do with employees, you may ask? Many of them are sitting in training sessions with no more desire to learn than all those reluctant students. Even your best employees are often sitting in training sessions thinking:

- This absolutely isn't the best use of my time.
- I could be finishing my project right now.
- I already know this stuff.
- I don't need to know this stuff.
- Such a waste just so they can check off a box to satisfy _____ (OSHA/ISO/Diversity Initiatives/HR—you fill in the blank).

Coaching, another favorite *best* and *beneficent* business practice, often fits the bill as well. "I am helping *you*. This is for *your* benefit. Your boss is paying me to change you. What are you going to do differently? Why didn't you try what we talked about last week?" Though coaches are rarely so direct. But just because they generally specialize in careful language, doesn't mean their goal isn't to *change you.*

Providing feedback is another activity that usually falls in the doing TO trap. Whether you are in the "They screwed up and I need to set them straight once and for all" camp or the feedback formula camp where you carefully spell out the observable behavior and its impact, if your goal is to change the other person, it's a TO goal. Even if you think that goal is safely hidden behind your eyes.

Managing others has TO written all over it! The word itself reeks of directing, corralling, and controlling others. The word "supervising" is almost as bad. Overseeing, spying, and evaluating. Not things we love done TO us!

And now for one of my favorites: impressing! I don't care if you are on a stage, running a meeting, or networking. If your goal is to *impress* others, you are doing TO. And you are likely to appear as pompous, arrogant, insecure, and/ or self-absorbed. (But if your goal is to *help* others, you will ask more questions, reach out to them, listen carefully, and show your interest in their needs. If you truly want to help, you will come across as sincere and helpful. Combine that with your expertise and you *will* impress!)

It's time to lighten up a bit and celebrate the WITH activities! Interestingly enough, there are really only four. You can listen, ask questions, answer questions, and offer to help.

"Wait a minute!" I hear you thinking. "How the heck do I do my job if I can only offer help and ask and answer questions?"

The answer starts with your mindset. If you adopt a partnership mindset, you will be able to set expectations, teach, coach, and provide feedback by working WITH your employees and not doing anything TO them.

There are really only four WITH activities.
You can listen, ask questions, answer questions, and
offer to help.

# Setting expectations WITH employees

When setting expectations, you and your employee have a mutual problem to solve: how to meet company and customer expectations.

"We need to do _____ by _____. As our expert in ____, I am thinking you are the one to ensure ____ for this project. Does that make sense to you? Is there any reason why you can't do that? Do you think you can meet that deadline? Is there anything you need from me?"

Contrast this exchange with a more traditional approach to setting clear and firm expectations. "I expect you to accomplish ____ by ____." "I need you to..." isn't much better.

Since many job positions almost predetermine employee roles on projects, setting expectations is often pretty straightforward and doesn't feel overbearing or controlling to the employee. Thus, I don't want to spend a lot of time talking about setting expectations here.

Nonetheless, look at the difference between those two examples. In the first, the boss states what is needed and asks questions. In the second, the boss tells the employee what to do.

# Teaching as a WITH activity

If you have ever been on the receiving end of unwanted instruction, you know the problem is that it is *unwanted*! And when it is unwanted, you don't listen well and you rarely learn. My big brother was always lecturing me. He wanted to teach me endlessly. Despite his good intentions, rarely was it something I wanted to learn and, even if the topic was interesting, his timing was usually off. My mind was elsewhere and the more he talked, the less I listened. The key to learning is being ready for it. We learn when given the opportunity to learn something we want to learn and at a time and place when we are ready to learn it.

My goal here is not to tell you how to teach, but to *make sure it is welcome* so it becomes an activity you do WITH others. In short, you need *permission* to teach.

If you need to teach a group of people, it is tough to ensure they all want to learn and are ready. But the least you can do is to be sure they understand why it is important and how they will benefit. Ask questions ahead of time so you can meet them where they are and tap into their concerns, desires, and fears. If they see the value, they will be more receptive and ready to work WITH you.

When dealing with individuals, it is much easier to shift from a TO approach to a WITH approach. Classic TO behavior would be to decide what your employee needs to learn, pick a time when you can teach, and then just tell them what you think they need to know. But you will be more successful if you take the WITH approach. One option is to seek a teachable moment—a situation when the employee is in the midst of an activity where what you have to teach them will make their job easier or their day more pleasant. Then offer to help. "Would you be interested in learning a faster way of doing that or how to avoid that problem next time?" "If so, is now a good time?"

Another option takes place after the fact. "I noticed that you put a lot of time into that project and still missed the deadline. Now maybe our expectations were unrealistic, but I was wondering if you would be interested in digging into what happened a bit with me. If I understood a little about how you approach a task like that, I might have some advice for how you could speed things up next time. Or perhaps Adrienne would be a better choice; she has a lot of experience on projects like that. Or maybe you have other ideas? Either way, I am happy to help."

Notice how these words factually state the situation. They lay no blame on the employee and, in the second example, actually suggest that the expectations may have been unrealistic given either the task, the capabilities of the employee, the level of resources that ended up being available, and maybe the amount of help you were able to provide along the way. They offer multiple options and leave the choice to the employee. There are no "shoulds"!

Once you gain permission to teach, that permission may or may not extend to future situations. This is a common problem for managers who are quick to assume they can teach anything in their bailiwick to anyone who reports to them and maybe anyone in the organization. They are the experts after all!

> The difference between doing TO and doing WITH can be as simple as gaining permission.

But assuming ongoing permission to teach is not a good assumption. Consider the employee who works really hard to improve their technique and the boss walks in, fails to notice or acknowledge the improvement, and simply starts correcting them once again. How would you feel if you were that employee?

On the flip side, perhaps your job requires a second language in which you are fluent but some coworkers clearly are not. A simple question can grant ongoing permission to teach. "Would you like me to correct any mistakes I hear so you can improve your Spanish?" A yes can make that an accepted part of your relationship. A no puts it off limits without additional permission.

Thus, ongoing permission depends on your relationship, the topic, similarity of circumstances, and how prior permission was given. However, there is never harm in asking, "Would you like some advice?"

# Coaching as a WITH activity

I'm often asked to coach employees by bosses with little concern as to whether the individual wants to be coached. To make matters worse, coaching is often a last-ditch effort in the mind of the manager to convert a bad hiring decision into a good investment or to pass the buck on a performance problem. In both cases, the goal is definitely to *fix* the employee. What could be more TO than that?!

In other cases, coaching is an investment in a promising employee. But even in those cases, the thinking and language often indicate that the employee is to be molded, developed—transformed even. The dutiful coach asks questions about how the manager would like the employee to behave differently, objectives are set, and then the coach, eager to impress, sets out to change the employee. A good coach can do a lot to turn this into a WITH experience, but can you see how the mindset is so wrong right off the bat? How everyone is thinking about what needs to be done TO the employee?

My coaching clients *ask* to be coached. Furthermore, they ask to be coached *by me*. Our relationship begins with their strong belief that they can learn from me. Our first face-to-face meeting solidifies that belief or we part ways. Thus, they are eager to get started. They couldn't be more receptive.

If the employee I am coaching isn't the CEO (rarely the case), I want to talk with the manager, but I don't want the manager deciding what needs to be done TO the employee by developing specific objectives with the manager. I learn about typical situations where the manager thinks the employee can do better, including where excellent employees could be *even* better, but my goal is to work WITH the employee. To understand where they would like to be better. To answer their questions. To offer advice. To challenge their assumptions. To give them ideas. But not to tell them what to do or how to think.

> Do WITH, not TO by listening, asking questions, and offering to help and you will be more successful in setting expectations, providing feedback, coaching, teaching, advising, etc.

Since my approach is so atypical, I don't call it coaching; I call it Clarity-on-Call—help when help is needed. I am not trying to change or do anything TO anyone. But guess what, my clients change! Remarkably, as a matter of fact. Because any changes they make are based on their own desire to learn and be better people and better at their jobs. They are totally willing to try new things and practice new behaviors because the motivation is all intrinsic. There is no pressure, no discipline, no reproaches. I don't do *anything* TO them.

# Providing feedback without doing it TO someone

As I'm sure you can see from the previous examples, whether by habit, language, or previous training, we tend to fall into doing TO behaviors. When giving feedback, the problem is particularly unfortunate because doing it TO someone instantly makes them defensive and upset, often angry, and unlikely to hear any of the helpful things we are trying to convey.

To be effective, not only must we keep our tendency to leap to assumptions and label employees at bay, but we must reject the urge to change them. If we try, we are most likely to fail. But if we work WITH them, we are far more likely to succeed.

Mindset is the lynchpin between doing TO and doing WITH. The distinction is clear and critical. If you think at all in terms of setting someone straight, making them see the light, disciplining them, fixing them, making yourself clear once and for all, or just changing them, you are already in the TO trap.

If you shift your mindset to the Disconnect Principle (all I know for certain is that something didn't go as I expected), you can more readily adopt a WITH mentality. You can ask about where things stand and what did or didn't happen and how that came to pass. You can listen empathically and sincerely. You can encourage questions and reflect on the answers. You can offer to help, offer ideas, and see if help is welcome.

> When someone is helpful and working WITH us,
> we feel supported and valued.

Your offer to help, by the way, does not mean that you are offering to solve the problem for them. That would be inappropriate except for time-restricted scenarios with the most junior employees and when significant risk is involved. You can offer advice, resources, and new ideas. But no matter what you wish to offer, it must be a sincere offer, not a TO intervention in disguise.

## Managing and supervising without doing it TO someone

The TO aspect of managing others is indisputable because managing incorporates all of the above. In addition, the manager is the boss and bosses boss by definition, even when they do it nicely. The hierarchical nature of the relationship includes an imbalance of power.

Managers and supervisors must be ever vigilant and self-aware to avoid slipping into TO behaviors.

> When you try to do something TO someone, you will likely fail. When you try to do something WITH someone, you are more likely to succeed.

We have all had people doing things TO us all our lives. When we are lucky, those activities align with our interests and the timing is good. When we are unlucky or the person doing TO us is tone-deaf, we end up annoyed, insulted, and angry. We don't learn. We shut down. We think more about how irritating the other person is than about what they are trying to tell us.

But the good news is that many classic TO activities become WITH activities simply by gaining permission.

| TO activities | WITH activities |
|---|---|
| • Teaching | • Listening |
| • Coaching | • Asking |
| • Giving feedback | • Answering |
| • Setting expectations | • Offering |
| • Holding accountable | |
| • Advising | |
| • Directing | |
| • Disciplining | |
| • Pressuring | |
| • Firing | |

Listen, ask, answer, and offer.

If your help is wanted and the timing is good, you can transform many TO activities into WITH activities by gaining permission and then proceed to help. If not, back off, propose another time, leave a standing offer, or try again later. And be prepared to take "no" for an answer!

The difference between doing TO and doing WITH can make the difference between whether your offer of help is accepted and successful or whether you irritate or insult the other party.

# Your thoughts, description, and offer

Before providing feedback, consider all three components:

Your Thoughts:

- Where are my thoughts?
- Is my goal to correct or do I really mean it when I say "We have a disconnect"?

Your Description of Behavior and Impact:

- Am I focused on specific, observable behavior and its impact?
- Have I purged all judgments, assumptions, and

generalizations from my brain?
- Am I honestly open to the possibility that I don't know the whole story and the reasons my expectations weren't realized?

Your Offer:

- Am I really on their side and eager to resolve the disconnect and/or prevent a recurrence WITH them?
- Am I offering to do something WITH them and not TO them?

If you can do this successfully, giving feedback need not be uncomfortable and will actually improve both performance and relationships.

| TYPICAL FEEDBACK | COMPONENTS OF FEEDBACK | EFFECTIVE FEEDBACK |
|---|---|---|
| Constructive feedback is needed. Someone needs fixing. | **A. YOUR THOUGHTS** ↓ | "We have a disconnect! All I know is that something didn't happen as I expected. Let's see how we can do better." |
| Result: Your body language, tone, and impromptu words will reveal your true thoughts. | | Result: You are seen wanting to make things better and knowing you may be part of the problem. |
| Generalizations (always, never), assumptions, multiple issues | **B. YOUR DESCRIPTION OF BEHAVIOR AND IMPACT** ↓ | Specific, observable behavior with clear explanation of impact and eager to hear the rest of the story. |
| Result: You will be wrong, you'll provoke, and may also overwhelm. | | Result: You are seen as honestly open and aware of how little you know. |
| Doing TO | **C. YOUR OFFER** | Doing WITH |
| Result: You will be insulting, not partnering. | | Result: You ask questions, offer help, let them choose if, how, and when. |

## Do you provoke or partner?

# Clear distinctions in summary

Doing TO is simply incompatible with the Disconnect Principle. We must shift our mindset if we are to embrace the Disconnect Principle and honestly work WITH others for improvement.

- Recognize the difference between doing TO and doing WITH.
- Pause before you interact in order to avoid the habitual TO approach.

Remember that if you try to do something TO another person, you are likely to fail. If you try to do something WITH another person, you are likely to succeed.

Your words and your body language will follow your thoughts, so take care of your thoughts, and be sure you are truly intent on working WITH the other person.

| The old way | With the Disconnect Principle |
|---|---|
| Doing TO as we:<br>    Teach<br>    Coach<br>    Give feedback<br>    Set expectations<br>    Hold accountable<br>    Advise<br>    Direct<br>    Discipline<br>    Pressure<br>    Terminate | → Doing WITH by:<br>    Listening<br>    Asking<br>    Answering<br>    Offering |
| You try to change others. | → You are clearly on their side. |
| Your certainty is disrespectful and insulting or annoying. | → You are driven by empathy and clarity. |
| You are a boss. | → You are a partner. |

And never forget:

Focus on the situation, *not* the person. Your goal is to fix the situation, *not* the person.

# 6.

# RETHINK ACCOUNTABILITY

---

Accountability is simply about establishing commitments and following through to deliver on those commitments so that the individuals in an organization can collectively sync their efforts to accomplish something no one could do alone. It's about teamwork and succeeding together.

Imagine what it would be like if we could embrace the essential spirit of accountability and banish all the pressure, punishment, and power that poisons it.

I can still picture the expression on the face of one of my bosses when I entered his office for a meeting that I knew instantly was about "holding me accountable." Jaw clenched to show that he was determined to be firm, maybe with a touch of *tough love* for *my* benefit. Prepared to tell me what I should do if I knew what was best for me. Eyes almost squinty to make sure I knew he was annoyed—but not so annoyed as to be unprofessional. Body rigid to protect himself from accidental friendliness.

It's kind of funny that I can picture Don so well, but I have no idea why he was so perturbed. There are two likely reasons for his exasperation, both related, both frequent. Either I wouldn't do something the way I was supposed to because I thought it was bureaucratic and ineffective or I had been too vocal in pushing back against decisions from on high.

I can think of lots of possible reasons, all of which could have earned me my most cherished corporate award: The Person Most Likely To Dispute Recognized Authorities. But, no, that I earned in a supervisory class where I kept asking questions and challenging the assumption that every Harvard study rolled out to impress was truly relevant.

Regardless of the provocation, I am quite certain that my boss hated trying to hold me accountable. Which is especially sad since I had a reputation for writing bug-free code and making all the deadlines that really mattered. I just wasn't good at doing things someone else's way when mine were working well. Don couldn't tell the difference apparently and was just trying to be a *dutiful* manager who kept all his employees *in line*. So he put on his boss mask, starched his body language, and held yet another unproductive conversation that made both of us uncomfortable.

Up until now, we've been talking about providing feedback and how important it is to purge judgmental thoughts that inappropriately presume guilt with insufficient evidence, to forget your superior position that makes you come across as condescending, and to work WITH your teammates—your direct reports as well as your peers and boss.

Now it's time to step back and consider the bigger picture: Accountability. The word "accountability" is loaded with negative connotations. Punitive comes to mind. So do pressure, coercion, and discipline. Most people squirm at the thought of holding others accountable.

It's sad because accountability is simply about teaming up for success.

It's not about performance ratings, promotions, titles, discipline, pressure, documenting transgressions, or the threat of termination. It's simply about agreeing on the plan and then working together to arrive at each port of call at the same time.

> Accountability is about collectively establishing commitments and delivering on those commitments so that the individuals can accomplish something no one could do alone.

Nonetheless, if you google "how to hold others accountable," you will get millions of hits—121 million the last time I checked. Those hits include numerous articles about how hard it is to hold others accountable and why. The titles include:

- "How to hold others accountable without blame"
- "How to hold others accountable without shame"
- "Hold people accountable without being a jerk"

- "Holding employees accountable: where most leaders fail"
- and many more.

But once again, the advice is all rules and tools, plus lists of vague objectives: clear expectations, clear feedback, clear consequences, clear consistency. (Isn't it funny how all those vague objectives include the word clear?) Among all those hits, you will find little to nothing about mindset, though I must admit I didn't read all 121 million articles!

From my personal experience, numerous audience responses, and client engagements, holding people accountable often invokes thoughts such as the following:

- I have to be firm, but *what if I wasn't clear*?
- They can be so manipulative and devious; I'll have to be alert.
- They are so oblivious; I question whether I can say anything that will make a difference.
- This could get ugly.
- It's time to put a stake in the ground!
- I must be armed against their excuses.
- They have brought this upon themselves.

The first bullet captures our self-doubt. Have I been clear? Am I being fair? I am always glad to see this reaction. It's really important, especially since we aren't as clear as we think we are. If you don't believe me, you really should read my book, *The Power of Clarity*. The first chapter is called *We Aren't As Clear As We Think We Are ... And It's*

*Costly*. Most people are quite shocked, and embarrassed, by the truth in that statement once they read the chapter.

How clear are you? For some clues, download the first chapter of *The Power of Clarity* now at DisconnectPrinciple.com

But the question of whether you are being fair also suggests that you are about to do something TO someone. If you've read the previous chapter of this book, you ought to find that a bit jolting. And, obviously, very little good comes of doing something TO someone else. It's actually quite hard to be unfair when you are truly doing your best to work WITH someone else.

> If you question whether you are being fair,
> you are probably about to do something TO
> someone.

The second and third bullets are indicative of falling into the trap of making assumptions and labeling your employee. If you have thoughts like these, not only are you about to do something TO someone, but you've already placed blame. It's an us vs. them situation in your brain. They are wrong and you are right.

The very fact that you are possibly on the verge of doing something TO someone suggests that you may have had some of the other thoughts on that bulleted list as well. You might not even realize it. You might be slow to admit it. Max, the client I mentioned in my opening story, certainly had some of those thoughts, but I don't think he would have said so had I asked. Instead, I believe he would have listed the specific, observable transgressions that he wanted to talk about. Notice that I called them *transgressions*, not *behaviors*. Max was certain his employee had done something wrong. Judgment had been passed. The employee was labeled irresponsible. And Max was ready to do something TO him. With that mindset, his carefully planned conversation was doomed to failure!

Our beliefs about and discomfort with accountability make accountability harder, not easier. The situation is exacerbated by the fact that most performance management systems have lost track of their mission. Instead of focusing on improving performance, they are more concerned with keeping score, discipline, and protecting the organization from lawsuits. The importance of rules and documentation supersedes collaboration.

How do we agree on what needs to be achieved and help each other get there? There are four critical factors:

- Setting expectations
- Providing feedback

- Following up
- Modeling desired behaviors.

We have already talked extensively about feedback and the importance of managing your thoughts, your description of behavior and its impact, and your offer (A, B, and C in the following diagram). In this chapter, we will talk about the other three bullets: setting expectations, following up, and modeling desired behaviors (D in the following diagram). In the next chapter, we will address employee development and perennial performance problems, which I prefer to think of as matchmaking (E in the diagram).

Empathic and pragmatic accountability

# Accountability partners rule

Have you ever had an accountability partner? People establish these relationships frequently to help them solidify their objectives, overcome obstacles, and increase focus. Accountability partners also help you understand what you are good at, how to leverage your natural talents and tendencies, and where you need to improve. They can point you in the right direction and challenge your assumptions. They can help you develop the systems and habits that make you more effective. In short, accountability partners can be enormously helpful. And they are unquestionably *on your side*! Someone you can trust to work WITH you!

> It's actually quite hard to be unfair when you are truly doing your best to work WITH someone else.

Do you think my client Max from the opening story was *unquestionably* on the same team as his employee when he walked into that conversation? Absolutely not! He was armed with foregone conclusions and prepared to discipline. His planned words were irrelevant. In his mind, he was right and his employee was a problem.

What most employees need in order to become the best version of themselves is an accountability partner, someone unmistakably on their team who is empathic, pragmatic, and willing to help them out. Other than a few misfits, whom you never should have hired in the first place, employees want to succeed. They want to feel good about their work and be proud of their accomplishments.

Every single employee needs to work constantly on improving their game. They need to take ownership of that improvement. They need to learn how to manage their time, sharpen their skills, and increase their focus. They need to develop systems and tools that work for them. They need to learn to recognize where they do and don't need additional structure and support and when to ask for help. They need to know that feedback is essential and not always given when needed, which means they need to learn to seek it. They need to know when to take risks and when to be patient. That's a lot to learn!

How do they learn? Through experimentation, reading books and articles, learning from others, and testing various tools and systems. Many develop great habits quite independently and need little support from others. Others really struggle. And to make matters worse, some of the tips they read on the Internet are really bad. Plus, trying out new techniques and tools, even just the good ones, can become an endless and deep drain on their time.

Some employees, unfortunately, don't recognize their struggles for what they are. They just feel frustration and tend to blame it on others or the organization as a whole. They don't realize that they need to take responsibility for their own personal development challenges.

And everyone has their struggles at some point. Everyone. Responsibilities shift. Pressures increase. Familiar systems change. Personalities clash. Disappointments cripple. Confidence suffers. Life interferes. Whether those struggles are ongoing or exceptions to the norm, that's when many employees could use an accountability partner.

As I said a few paragraphs earlier, every single employee needs to work constantly on improving their game and they need to take ownership of that improvement. They need to learn to manage themselves. To do that, the last thing they need is a boss who is quick to see mistakes as personal flaws and missed expectations as proof of failure rather than a tiny clue in a complex puzzle. They need an accountability partner. So don't be a boss; be a partner! After all, you are on the same team!

# The right mindset

Once again, mindset matters, arguably above all else. A good manager *partners* for success:

- Partners encourage us to develop self-awareness and take charge of our own development.
- Partners help us develop necessary knowledge, skills, structure, and systems by *offering* advice and ideas, not by trying to change us.
- Partners let us know where things stand so we can use our best judgment and problem-solving skills to make improvements and amends. They provide honest and timely feedback. "Would you like some ideas on how that could have been (even) better? Is now a good time to talk?"
- Partners don't think in terms of negative and positive, just facts. "Let's be sure we understand where things stand so we/you can decide on next steps."
- Partners don't convert missed expectations into character flaws.
- Partners embrace the Disconnect Principle when something doesn't happen as expected by realizing that all that's certain is that something didn't happen

as expected. They then enter into an open, honest, empathic discussion ready to learn the current state of affairs and figure out what should be done next to move things forward and/or to prevent a recurrence.
- Partners don't try to fix the employee. They work WITH, not TO.

In short, a partner would never think in terms of:

- Holding our feet to the fire.
- Setting us straight.
- Fixing us.
- Making us toe the line.
- Telling us that it's "my way or the highway."

That's not what any of us want or need. Nor is it effective. And should words such as those ever enter your head, you've already lost. Lost the opportunity to increase the odds of success. Lost the respect of others. Lost a piece of your own humanity. And undoubtedly created a lot of doubt and anxiety for yourself.

> The minute you consider "fixing" others,
> you have likely lost some of their respect,
> the opportunity to help,
> and a piece of your own humanity.

How did accountability become laden with punitive

connotations? I don't know, but it's common, horrific, and inexcusable. Always remember:

- You and your employees are on the same side.
- They want to succeed.
- You need them to succeed.
- Many traditional images of accountability threaten success.
- The point is to partner for success.

Pressure from you simply doesn't help. And it's so much easier to simply say, "We have a disconnect. This is what I expected. What were you expecting? How can we make this work?"

# Setting expectations that stick

How you go about setting expectations can make a big difference in the likelihood of success as well as your relationships with your employees. Clarity and collaboration are key. Both are in the spirit of everything we've talked about and both make accountability easy. Let's start with clarity.

I know you know that clarity is important. What you may not know is that what most people think is clear really isn't clear at all. (Even the word "clarity" is incredibly unclear!) I wrote the book on clarity, *The Power of Clarity*, and I certainly can't repeat all of that here, so let me give you one tip. Be specific! You and your employee both need to agree on what success looks like. You both need to be able to explain exactly what will be different when you are done and how it will unleash next steps.

Learn more about *The Power of Clarity* by reading the introduction. Go to DisconnectPrinciple.com now.

In setting expectations, be specific! Both parties must be able to explain exactly what will be different when they are done and how it will unleash next steps.

While clarity is essential to *what* expectations are set, collaboration is essential to *how* they are set. As mentioned when discussing setting expectations as a WITH activity, it isn't difficult and goes something like this:

- This is what needs to be done.
- Due to a project deadline, it looks like we need it by the end of this month.
- I think you (and your team) are perfectly suited for this.
- Does that make sense? Does this sound reasonable?
- Are we in agreement?
- Excellent! Let's check back when you reach step X.

With this approach, you are not telling someone what to

do using your boss persona. Instead, you are leaving room for questions, clarification, negotiation, and agreement. And don't fall into the trap of looking for a quick yes and assume you really are in agreement. As I said above, it is imperative that your employee's description of what will be different when done matches yours.

> Clarity is essential to *what* expectations are set; collaboration is essential to *how* they are set.

The third bullet above gives you an opportunity to call attention to their track record, how you value their contribution, and how much you appreciate being able to hand off such an important task to them. I'm not suggesting you flood them with praise like bribery, in case that's what you are thinking. I'm merely suggesting that each bullet offers a great opportunity to express a little sincere appreciation.

Notice that the last bullet concludes by clarifying how you will work together on this. Spend some time identifying the steps of the process you and they will use. Do you want to be sure you have an opportunity to provide input on step 2? Do you want to check progress on step 4? The point is to make a conscious decision as to where you and your employee believe your input will be most effective and necessary and then establish a promise to reconnect at that point.

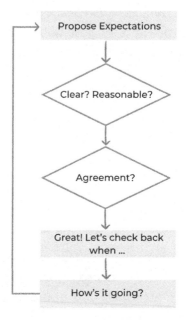

Setting expectations and checking in

# What does checking in look like?

If you were as clear as I'd hope when setting expectations, checking in would include three parts.

First, you would address whatever you agreed needed to be addressed when you set expectations and scheduled this check-in. I hope you didn't agree to check in just because it was Monday or the end of the month. I hope you and your employee were far more specific than that about what would be complete and why your input would be appropriate. Did you want to confirm or compare notes on the objectives your employee had established for an important decision? Did you want to authorize resources? Perhaps you wanted to see how they have planned to approach the project overall? Or check whether they had identified risks and made reasonable mitigation plans? Or maybe you want to see if you have any risks to add to their list? (For much more detail on delegating and when to check in on employees, read my book *The Power of Clarity*.)

Second, you would ask about obstacles and offer support. You do this by asking more specific questions than "How's it going?" This is where partnering for success comes in. Are they comfortable with these responsibilities and the deadline? Do they need help?

Now is also a good time for what I call "defensive planning" questions:

- What is going to bite us?
- What are we taking for granted?
- What have we yet to learn that is really important to our success?
- What have you learned in the last week that has you thinking differently about this project and next steps?
- How do you know you will finish on time?

People rarely ask enough questions of this kind. These questions teach the art of anticipating and preventing problems. They encourage thoughtful initiative rather than blindly following plans, processes, or orders. And they are far more powerful than turning to the plan to see how many items have been or can be checked off the list.

When we focus on the check-off approach, we are abdicating responsibility for results in favor of measuring activity. We are also making the often-disastrous assumption that the plan was perfect to start with. Checking off completed tasks creates the illusion of progress. But enough on how to manage projects, since that's not the topic of this book. Maybe it will be the topic of the next book I write.

The third part of your check-in involves resetting expectations. Plans change—or, at least, you should be watching for the need for them to change. Thus, at each check-in, it's time to determine whether expectations still make sense. Are they still reasonable? Do you still have agreement on this? Have you established another check-in point?

Notice that all three steps are WITH activities where you collaborate for success.

# You, the exemplar

I did not write this book just for bosses, but if you are one, you need to take your role as an exemplar seriously. If you want your employees to take their commitments seriously, you need to take your commitments seriously. You must model the behavior you wish to see in your employees. Nothing less than your integrity depends on it. That means you must:

- Keep your promises
- Meet your deadlines
- Ask for help when you need it
- Develop your own self-awareness
- Seek feedback
- Admit and apologize for your mistakes
- Make changes, not excuses
- And embrace the Disconnect Principle and all the mindsets and behaviors described in this book.

You absolutely cannot expect your employees to exhibit these behaviors if you don't. You are the exemplar. You and all of the other leaders in the organization.

Get the Disconnect Principle Mindshift Summary to hang on your wall. Go to DisconnectPrinciple.com now.

# Clear distinctions in summary

Accountability partners don't hold anyone's feet to the fire. It is uncomfortable for all and accomplishes little. Partner for success by following all the mindshifts suggested in this book.

| The old way | With the Disconnect Principle |
|---|---|
| Tell employees what to do and when. | → Set expectations collaboratively. |
| Require regular reports from all. | → Check in as agreed when you established expectations. |
| Check off tasks as completed. | → Ask provocative questions that anticipate and prevent problems. |
| Provide constructive or corrective feedback when needed. | → Insist that all feedback is constructive and dismiss the positive/negative dichotomy. |
| Watch for evidence that confirms your fears and assumptions about the employee's performance. | → Banish assumptions, judgments, and generalizations. |
| Hold them accountable by applying appropriate pressure. | → Be quick to recognize that "We have a disconnect!" |
| Fix the employee. | → Fix the situation. |
| Do TO. | → Do WITH. |
| Clarify consequences. | → Truly partner for success. |

# 7.

# THE MOTHER OF ALL DISCONNECTS

---

It's time to talk about the biggest and most destructive disconnect of all:

> A mismatch between what the organization needs and what the employee is willing and able to offer is the mother of all disconnects.

No one wins if that match is poor. If the employee isn't able to deliver or if the employee just doesn't particularly want to deliver, the employee loses, the manager loses, the team loses, and the organization loses.

Mismatched employees not only struggle to succeed, they also struggle to find enjoyment in their work and the way they are required to spend their precious time. The result is anxious nights and tedious days.

The managers of those employees suffer because underperforming team members not only reduce the team's ability as a whole to meet expectations, but they also consume a disproportionate share of the manager's time and energy. In addition, managers often lose the respect and confidence of their team if they are seen as not dealing with underperformance adequately.

Team members are affected negatively as well. They are frequently forced to pick up the slack. Watching a coworker flounder is distracting, if not frustrating and painful. And in some cases, employees are led astray when they see what others are "getting away with." A morale killer is an apt description.

The organization as a whole suffers when their people suffer and when their ability to deliver is hampered. No one wins.

I often say that the #1 responsibility of a manager is to create clarity. Nowhere is this more true than the clarity needed to match employees to the needs of the organization.

In response to a survey I gave to a client organization recently, one of the managers said that the thing he liked least about managing people was that it took so much time away from doing real work. This is a super common problem: competent employees with solid track records are promoted to management positions without recognizing the enormous shift that entails.

Individual contributors produce, often with a fair amount of autonomy. Their accomplishments are usually pretty tangible and a clear source of pride.

A manager, on the other hand, must get that sense of accomplishment and pride through the accomplishments of others to a large extent. They may be the boss, but they often actually have less autonomy than their direct reports. The way they spend their time is different. The skills they need and must be eager to develop are different.

Anyone who thinks managing people takes away from "real work" is still thinking like an individual contributor. This is not uncommon and some individual contributors struggle significantly when making this shift. If an employee who acquires supervisory responsibilities for the first time can't make the shift or loses interest in trying to make the shift, you've got the ultimate disconnect.

There are a number of reasons we end up suffering this common mistake so often. One is that we simply tend to promote strong employees without digging deeper. They are handy. They are present. We trust them.

But let's not put this all on the manager. Employees often pursue greater status and pay without digging deeper into their own interests and skills. They strive to become supervisors and managers with little understanding of how that will affect their lives. And I do mean lives! If your job no longer gives you the satisfaction of individual accomplishment or the opportunity for the in-depth problem solving that you crave, it will change your life. Some people absolutely have to find replacements outside work or they drive family and friends crazy.

> I often say that the #1 responsibility of a manager is to create clarity. Nowhere is this more true than the clarity needed to match employees to organizational needs.

A mismatch between employee and position is the ultimate disconnect. No one's expectations will be met! No one will be happy, satisfied, or successful. That will be true for the employee, their coworkers, and the manager, as well as the organization as a whole.

# Employment as matchmaking

A good match is a win-win agreement between two people who have something to offer each other. That's the fair, respectful, doing WITH approach to employment.

A doing TO approach positions the employer as the person with the power and the employee as someone lucky to have a job. It's a lousy way to run a relationship.

To create and maintain an honest, two-way negotiation and doing WITH approach, both sides have responsibilities. What is needed is honest discussion between manager and employee and introspection on the part of the employee with the intent of establishing a win-win match.

### E. Developing a win-win match

Manager's responsibility:
- Our direction is evolving.
- You are evolving.
- Where do your passions lie?
- This is what we need.
- Is there a strong overlap between our needs and your knowledge, skill, and passions or is it time to part ways?
- Agreement reached.

Employee's responsibility:
- Am I passionate about my work?
- Do I understand what they need me to learn and do differently?
- Am I interested in and determined to learn those things?
- Is there a strong overlap between their needs and my knowledge, skill, and passions or is it time to part ways?
- Agreement reached.

Responsibilities for developing a win-win match

This diagram shows the responsibilities of the manager and of the employee and the interplay between the two. Notice that this isn't a top-down decision by the employer about what's best for the organization and how to use the employee. And it certainly isn't the old school model: "I'm the boss. I decide who to hire and fire." No, in this approach, there are two equal and distinct players. It's a respectful partnership. It's a negotiation as exists in most honorable business dealings. One offers an opportunity and the other offers capabilities. The agreement to work together is mutual, as is the agreement to part ways.

You might think this is unrealistic, but consider what this mindset does for you. The key here is that the issue is the match between the role and the employee. Just as you can talk about disconnects without getting into personal attributes, failures, or blame, you can talk about the match between role and employee without getting into personal attributes, failures, or blame.

> Just as you can talk about disconnects without getting into personal attributes, failures, or blame, you can talk about a mismatch (the ultimate disconnect) between employee and position without getting into personal attributes, failures, or blame.

As the people and organizational needs evolve, the match must also evolve. If the match doesn't seem to be working out, it's time to revisit the match or agree to part ways. Focus on the match. Don't judge the person. Either you can find a match between an organization's needs and the employee's interests and capabilities or you can't.

"We've tried several times now to figure out how you can _____ (meet deadlines/avoid mistakes/ manage employees without drama—whatever the need that doesn't seem to be a good match for the employee, being as specific as possible). I think we are at the point where we have to ask whether responsibility for _____ is a good fit for you."

In this statement, you are recognizing a problematic track record despite several problem-solving conversations about individual disconnects. And it's all about the match, not their personal characteristics or failings.

You still want to collaborate for the best solution and you don't want to do TO, so you might go on to say:

"If you think it is a good match, help me understand how you see the situation. How do you see this coming together? What do you think can fundamentally change what's happening?"

And then:

"Most important of all, are you truly interested in developing those skills, awareness, and habits. If it isn't interesting enough to you to ensure a serious investment of your effort and time, we need to shift these responsibilities to someone else. If you don't really want to learn these things, why torture yourself?"

Or maybe it isn't about skill, but more about style and values:

"It seems you don't like or respect our _____ (values/ management approach/culture/ processes/strategy). I can understand that. Some people think we are _____ (too idealistic/cautious/lean/aggressive/slow). Nonetheless, this is our way of thinking and operating. I think the question is whether you can embrace it? Can you see yourself enthusiastically working within the constraints of our organization? If not, it doesn't make sense for you to work here."

# If only it were so simple

Wouldn't it be nice if you could just take a few measurements and immediately see the overlap between what you need and what any employee is willing and able to offer?

I know of no such tool, so you will have to talk with each other, provide honest feedback regarding how things are going, be really clear about what the organization needs, and ask about the kinds of activities that motivate and challenge the employee.

Let's look at some examples of disconnects and how the ensuing conversation might go.

Consider the case where a recent change in responsibilities started the disconnects (e.g., a promotion):

> "It seems to me you were happy before you became _____ and you did really well as _____. Luckily, our current staffing situation would allow you to resume that work and then we could take this burden away."

If a subset of responsibilities just isn't a good fit:

> "Let's plan on removing these responsibilities. I'll dig into our staffing needs and see whether there are other needs you might be well positioned to fulfill. Keep in mind though that I can't guarantee a full-time position at your current salary level once we remove these responsibilities."

If the employee suddenly wants to learn something that has seemed of little interest in the past:

> "I am sorry, but if you aren't a good match for that, ignoring that mother of all disconnects would be a mistake for both of us. You won't be happy and we won't be happy. If you have other ideas of what you might do for us, I am happy to consider them, but this particular issue has been too disruptive for too long and I'm considering this a final decision."

Notice again that this isn't about their failure as a person or even their ability to deliver. It is all about whether there is a mismatch between position and employee. Every mismatch causes trouble and prolonging the pain helps no one. Have I already said that? Probably. And I will likely say it again because it is so important.

---

Focus on the match, *not* on the person.
Fix the match, *not* the person.

---

This approach does not preclude adding plenty of encouragement related to what the employee excels at, how much people like them, and where you see opportunities for them elsewhere. Some people who are really good with people are naturals for positions dealing with people. That doesn't mean they are good at making deadlines or being detail-oriented. People who are really good at problem-solving are naturals for positions that require problem solving, but often poor choices for managing people. Few people make a smooth transition from solving technical or physical problems to solving people problems. (I consciously made that transition myself. The result is practically a whole new branch of management art and science focused on teaching knowledge workers and leaders how to create the kind of clarity that will make them and their coworkers more productive, confident, and empowered. That's why I wrote *The Power of Clarity*.)

Curious about *The Power of Clarity*? Download the introduction now at DisconnectPrinciple.com

# Employees are adults

The matchmaking approach fits well with our rethinking of accountability in the previous chapter. It also puts more responsibility on the employee. In this model, employees can't just "do the job." They need to:

- Take ownership of their career.
- Examine their interests, understand what makes them tick, and figure out where their talent ignites their energy and compels them to contribute.
- Listen and seek feedback so they know how well they are delivering and what they need to learn.

- Develop their self-management skills and figure out when to seek additional structure, systems, and support to ensure their own success.
- Explore the overlap between what's best for them and their employer's needs.
- Recognize when the match simply isn't there if they aren't happily meeting expectations and justifying their paycheck.
- Know when it is time to part ways and find an alternative that makes them happier and more successful.

Many employees need help with these responsibilities, starting with being sure they understand that these *are* their responsibilities!

I remember being told more than once over my many jobs that I should take ownership of my career. I don't think I ever really did that until shortly before I left the corporate world to start my own business. It seems to me I only thought in terms of promotions, salary, and which job I might want. I don't think I ever got the feeling there was room for negotiation. I didn't think in terms of being responsible for my job satisfaction and its alignment with my passions. UNTIL, I had a boss who helped me start understanding and recognizing important distinctions such as the difference between:

- Being an individual contributor and being a manager
- Being the visible head of the team and being the staff person behind the scenes but critical to the

team's success
- Being strategic and being tactical and detail-oriented
- Being a craftsman and being more cerebral
- Being eager to follow orders and being driven to find the best path.

Once I started seeing distinctions such as these, I started thinking less about promotions and what I would be allowed to do and more about what I really liked doing and choices that would be good for me. That boss did me a tremendous favor, a favor every employee deserves. When employees understand what makes for a win-win match and their role in achieving one, it is so much easier for managers to work WITH them to create and maintain a good match.

# Perennial performance problems

Managers often tell me that their problems with giving feedback only occur with immature or problematic employees and that the performance problems never end. My first responses: Are you sure you are not provoking them and making them defensive with corrective advice and judgmental thoughts? Are you doing TO? Are you setting them straight?

Or are you truly embracing the Disconnect Principle, exploring circumstances empathically, offering to help, and negotiating as equals?

If the latter, then the next step is some serious conversations about the employee's interests and contributions relative to what the organization needs as explained earlier. It won't necessarily be easy, but it can be pretty straightforward and you shouldn't feel miserable if you keep your focus on the match.

> "We really appreciate your ability to do X, but as you know, you've struggled to do Y and doing X is not a full-time position. As you also know, we had you try Z for a while, but that really wasn't of interest to you."

Be honest and direct. Never cloud these conversations with artificial hope. People hear what they want to hear. Give them false hope and they will miss the real message.

Perennial problems should never be allowed to become perennial, of course. An employee who repeatedly misses deadlines despite your joint efforts to prevent that needs to know they aren't a good fit for the position.

For example, a manager who is constantly at the center of drama despite repeated discussions as to what is going on needs to know that the mutual stress and confrontation involved in such situations points to a mismatch between what the position demands and what the manager is ready, willing, and able to do. And unless the manager can think of something to resolve the tension that has yet to be tried, it looks like everyone would be better off parting ways.

Now let's look at some specific problems that my clients

have found challenging and see how the Disconnect Principle and its vital mindsets relate. In these examples, there is no blame, no judgment, and no threats. The focus is on simple facts, the requirements of the role and the match between the employee and the role. There is no doing TO. There are offers to help. And yet, the consequences are clear as well.

Keep in mind that as long as you remember that this isn't about failure or personal characteristics, it's easier to discuss almost anything. A mismatch of employee and position is the ultimate disconnect. Can it be resolved? It is as much the employee's responsibility to come up with a solution as it is the manager's. Ideally, an employee who detracts more than they add recognizes that fact (with your help and honesty) and knows when it is time to leave.

**An employee has different standards than I do—they work hard but don't produce adequately.**

Expectations that are carefully set specify what must be different when the employee is done. What exactly does success look like? What criteria will be used to determine success? Use standard criteria when possible. If those standards don't exist, define what constitutes adequate performance. Be specific.

> "Thank you for working so hard on this. I owe you an apology. I screwed up. I obviously didn't make my expectations clear. Let's sit down a little later and see if we can come up with clearer criteria for what success looks like."

**My employees complain that expectations are never clear enough.**

They are probably right. (Read *The Power of Clarity*, especially the first chapter: *We Are Not As Clear As We Think We Are ... And It's Costly*.)

You can read that chapter now for free. Download it from DisconnectPrinciple.com

What makes you think expectations were clear in the first place? Can you point to clear specifications of what must be different when they are done? And are your employees able to articulate those concrete, tangible outcomes that match your expectations, including important timing and methods?

Did you actually reach agreement during the process of setting expectations or did you do it TO them?

Did you also establish a check-in point up front and at each subsequent follow up session so you could provide input at suitable points and maintain your confidence in their progress?

If, despite this level of clarity, your employee perpetually complains of unclear expectations, you need to ask questions. Put on your Disconnect Principle hat and say: "When you tell me expectations were unclear, I don't doubt that is possible, but we need to know more specifically what was unclear so we can prevent this from happening again. Let's take this last example. Help me understand what you thought was expected."

As with all complaints, after you've tried everything to resolve the issue, you and your employee have to ask yourselves whether the match is a good fit. It might be time to part ways.

**Employee frequently reacts defensively.**

Are you making them defensive? Are you trying to correct them, even if just in your mind? Is your feedback focused on specific, observable behavior or straying into judgment, assumptions, generalizations, and personal characteristics? Do you do TO, rather than WITH when you try to resolve problems? Are you a boss or an accountability partner?

If you have tried all of the above, it's time to talk with the employee about their reaction. Don your Disconnect Principle hat, pick one recent instance when defensiveness was a problem, and say:

"When I tried to give you feedback just now, you replied that _____ (it wasn't your fault/I wasn't being fair—fill in the blank). I know I don't always choose my words well, but I want to learn and I want to be able to work with you better. I certainly didn't mean for you to react that way. Can we talk about what happened?"

You are searching for one of two outcomes. The first possibility is you learn something about yourself and how you come across to this employee. When they start to give you that feedback, which might be pretty painful, a perfect response to prevent *you* from becoming defensive is, "Tell me more"! Learn what you can. Maybe you can agree on some code words that keep the door open and avoid defensiveness in the future.

The second possibility is that you get a chance to help this employee develop greater self-awareness as to why they react the way they do and whether they'd be interested in knowing how you handle defensiveness. Share the tip of saying, "Tell me more." You may even get a chance to remind them that breathing before overreacting is a really tough skill to learn but one that is important to being an effective employee since we can't afford to be annoyed as often as people say annoying things.

**Employee is not very self-aware.**

"Not very self-aware" is an example of labeling personal characteristics and isn't specific enough to trigger improvement. Pick one situation, put your Disconnect Principle hat on so you are ready to be open and honest, and explain the specific behavior and impact.

"When you did _____ two weeks ago, I tried to explain the implications and, as I recall, we had a really awkward conversation. When you did it again today, I tried to talk with you about it and that too turned uncomfortable. Despite two awkward conversations, I can't see that we have accomplished anything. I don't know what went wrong, but here is the situation. We have to be able to work together better than that. I have to be able to give you feedback, and you have to be able to listen and work with me on necessary changes. Now I know I am not perfect and I probably set you off with something I said, but we need to sort this out. So how about we start over and figure this out? How about we get together tomorrow and take a look together at what happened?"

Also keep in mind that self-awareness is never a one-sided issue. I've never met anyone who couldn't be more self-aware, have you?

**Employee always complains about others and processes instead of figuring out how to get their job done despite current constraints and inefficiencies.**

Let's break this one into its four pieces:

1. Employee complains
2. About others
3. And processes
4. Instead of figuring out how to get their job done within the current constraints and inefficiencies.

Now let's address them one at a time.

1. Employee complains:

"Do you have a specific disconnect you would like to discuss or are you just venting?"

If venting: "That's fine, but do you really need me for that?"

2. About others:

"Do you have a specific disconnect in mind?"

"Have you discussed it with the person central to the issue?"

"Remember to focus on fixing the situation, not the person."

3. About processes (rules, etc.):

"Do you have a specific disconnect or obstacle in mind?"

"Is it within our authority to fix?"

If the issue is known (on hold, underway, or scheduled): "Are you aware that we are _____?"

If a new issue: "How about raising that issue by _____ (whatever mechanism exists or makes sense in this situation to bring attention to a new issue)?"

4. Instead of figuring out how to get their job done:

"It sure will be nice when that's resolved, won't it!"

"In the meantime, we all have to work within the constraints and limitations surrounding us. If you aren't willing and able, we may have the ultimate disconnect!"

If the complaints continue:

> "We've discussed these same concerns of yours several times. You know that some of those issues are either being addressed or have been put on hold due to other priorities. In the meantime, we have to operate with our existing employees and processes. I am happy to help you figure out how to do that, but talking about these same issues repeatedly is a waste of time for both of us. If you simply can't work within the current constraints, I think we have the mother of all disconnects—a mismatch between what the organization needs and what you are willing and able to provide."

**If and when any conversation just plain goes wrong, recognize the disconnect!**

> "Let's stop. We have a disconnect."

And if appropriate:

> "This isn't the way I expected this conversation to go. Think we can start over? Think you can help me understand what went wrong? I really want to figure this out. Would you like to try now or would it be better to try again later?"

Just remember, you do no one any favors by keeping someone in a position where they can't succeed, aren't happy, or are making others miserable, including you. If the two of you can't get to the bottom of the issues, be done with each other. Life is short. When it's time to move on, move on.

> The more ingrained in your culture the idea of disconnects, matchmaking, and the dual responsibilities for the match, the better for all.

When done well, both sides recognize the mismatch and agree to make changes or part ways.

- Managers feel fair, honest, and humane.
- The talk and solutions are pragmatic, but still empathic.
- Employees feel respected, grow professionally and personally, and know when it is time to move on.

Remember, you are not passing judgment. You are not criticizing. You are not doing anything TO them. You are simply sharing what you need and what you see, exploring mutually satisfactory options together, helping where you can, and searching hard for a good match that is truly win-win.

# Clear distinctions in summary

Avoid the ultimate disconnect: a mismatch between the requirements of a position and the employee's knowledge, skill, and enthusiasm for fulfilling the demands of that position. When everyone shifts their mindsets to matchmaking, the following transformations occur:

| The old way | With the Disconnect Principle |
|---|---|
| "You are lucky to have a job" → | A win-win relationship |
| Boss dictates → | Boss learns about position and employee |
| Employee suffers → | Employee chooses |
| Boss rules → | Honest, two-way exploration of match/mismatch |
| Boss fires → | Separation decisions are mutual, logical, empathic, and based on the mismatch |

When each employee is well suited to their position, everyone wins. When any employee is a mismatch, people suffer, time is wasted, enthusiasm wanes, trust and respect dwindle, and cynicism spreads. Hire carefully and ferret out the mismatches quickly. When disconnects are found, tweak the role or guide the employee toward a more suitable position, within or beyond the organization, as soon as possible. Make matchmaking an open, honest, and revealing exploration between equals in search of a win-win relationship. A mismatch between employee and position is the ultimate disconnect.

# 8.

# CONNECTING THROUGH DISCONNECTS

---

Disconnects are everywhere. Every minute of every day something doesn't happen as you expected.

You can get mad, frustrated, ornery, and cynical. You can brood, blame, and build a case against someone. You can draw copious conclusions and commiserate with others. You can try to ignore it and suffer the consequences later. But why would you?

Why would you let a simple disconnect spoil your day or a relationship?

The power of the Disconnect Principle is that it frees you of all those enervating emotions and preconceived notions, and opens your mind to respectful, empathic listening and pragmatic problem solving. It allows you to give the benefit of the doubt and treat others as partners on the same team and with a shared goal. It makes you suitably humble and shows that you know you don't know everything about a situation.

When you embrace the simple disconnect mindset, you can explore what did or didn't happen without anger or judgment and then determine reasonable next steps. You are less likely to make assumptions about the personal characteristics and motives of others. Your use of the feedback formula will be sincere and more effective as you refer to specific, observable behavior and its impact. And when you enter problem-solving mode, you are more likely to do WITH and not TO. In short, the Disconnect Principle shifts your focus from the person to the situation and from "managing" people to managing situations and the match between the person and the position.

> The power of the Disconnect Principle is that it frees you from enervating emotions and preconceived judgments. It puts the focus on the situation, not the person. It treats all parties as equals deserving of respect and fair treatment.

The Disconnect Principle is perfect for dealing with immediate problems as they occur regardless of who is involved. Seriously! It doesn't matter whether the confusion or missed expectations are between a boss and a direct report, a direct report and a boss, or two coworkers. Rank and power are irrelevant.

"I think we have a disconnect," is a signal to anyone, especially those familiar with the Disconnect Principle, that it's time to take stock without blame. Where are we? How do we make things work?

It applies to little simple problems such as a boss's lack of clarity.

"I think we have a disconnect. Will you tell me more specifically what needs to be different when I am done?" (Those of you who have read *The Power of Clarity* recognize the magic in that question!)

It applies to uncomfortable conversations.

"When I tried to explain the consequences of what you just did, you didn't react as I expected, or at least not as I'd hoped. I think we have a disconnect. Can we try that again?"

It applies to big problems and makes it easier for people to admit mistakes.

"Holy Schmoly! I think we are about to suffer the consequences of a humongous disconnect! I'm sorry, but I was off track. Let's sit down and see if we can sort out what to do next."

It applies to perennial performance problems.

"I think we have a disconnect. Let's talk about these responsibilities in terms of how they fit with your interests and capabilities, especially your interests. It helps neither of us if I am hoping you will do something you simply don't care to do."

It transcends the workplace and can be used to deal with disappointments that involve family and friends.

"I'm sorry. I think we have a disconnect. I think I just said something regrettable. How about I shut up and let you explain."

It even works with contractors and suppliers, volunteer workers, and community issues.

"We clearly have a disconnect. Help me understand where things stand and what you are suggesting or trying to do."

# The coolest thing about the Disconnect Principle

But you know one of the coolest things about the Disconnect Principle?

It makes you communicate more carefully and listen more empathically. It makes you treat others with more respect. And, as a result, you learn more. You learn more about others *and* you learn more about *yourself*. You build trust and understanding. You also feel better about yourself and more confident. You can shed that boss persona that maybe never fit you particularly well anyway. And you build stronger relationships and stronger teams. All while developing pragmatic solutions.

It helps anyone who has been put on the defensive repeatedly by badly camouflaged judgments feel respected, heard, and given a chance to tell their side of the story. It makes it easier for everyone to recognize, admit, and learn from mistakes and shortcomings, especially *when their boss is doing likewise.*

It also helps people resolve peer-to-peer disagreements and disappointments so they don't fester or require wasteful escalation to higher powers.

It encourages informal feedback and bottom-up feedback as it renders power structures irrelevant and unnecessary.

If that's not a win-win-win, I don't know what is!

From working with hundreds of clients, I know the best-informed, best-intentioned people struggle with many of the same problems when trying to hold others accountable and provide feedback. But now that you have read this book, every single one of these classic issues should look different to you.

- How to avoid making others defensive
- How to deal with different standards of performance
- How to make consequences clear
- What to do about people with inadequate self-awareness or maturity
- How to prevent overreacting and underreacting
- What to do when expectations may have been unclear
- How to handle excuses
- How to let employees go without feeling mean or unfair.

Go forth and embrace the Disconnect Principle. Use it to simply, empathically, and unemotionally:

- Unravel missed expectations by acknowledging you know little about what actually happened.
- Purge judgmental thoughts, preconceived notions, and blame.
- Stay focused on observable behavior and its impact.
- Work sincerely WITH others to listen, learn, and solve problems, and avoid doing TO them.
- Be an accountability partner and fire your boss persona.
- Focus on the match between employees and their position, not personal characteristics and failures.
- Treat others with respect.

When something doesn't happen as you expected, all you know for certain is that something didn't happen as you expected. You don't know what actually happened or didn't happen and you certainly don't know why. Fix the situation, *not* the person!

> Would you like a compilation of all of the sample dialog provided in this book? If so, go to DisconnectPrinciple.com and download The Disconnect Principle Dialog Collection.

As this mentality permeates your culture, the whole

atmosphere shifts. That old-fashioned, top-down, controlling power model will be replaced by more people stepping up and taking charge of their responsibilities, resolving disconnects, and making things happen. You will see more signs of mutual respect, less condescension, and employees taking ownership of their careers, including their decisions to leave.

Embrace the Disconnect Principle and you will be happier, calmer, less frustrated, more successful, and more effective in dealing with the multitude of unmet expectations and the people involved. The Disconnect Principle has the power to change the way you manage people, particularly your approach to setting expectations, providing feedback, holding others accountable, and performance management.

# Clear distinctions in summary

The Disconnect Principle has the power to transform.

| The old way | | With the Disconnect Principle |
| --- | --- | --- |
| Feeling inadequate | → | Feeling confident |
| Fear and avoidance | → | Timely action |
| Burying the negatives in comfortable fluff | → | Being clear and direct |
| Truly painful conversations | → | Mutually agreeable problem solving |
| Continued or worsening problems | → | Performance enhancing commitment and more effective behavior |
| Tiptoeing around problem employees | → | Witnessing real improvement |
| Damaged relationships | → | Strong, trusting relationships |
| Adversaries | → | Invaluable partners |
| Feeling miserable | → | Being empathic |
| Perennial problems | → | Pragmatic action |

Here is your chance to be your compassionate, humane, fair self with greater ease and less effort. Embrace the Disconnect Principle today!

Please take 5 minutes to leave me a review. It helps other people to decide if they want to read the book, and I'll be eternally grateful. If you're reading on Kindle, just scroll to the end of the book to find the link so you can post a review. If you're reading the paperback, please go to your favorite online bookstore to post a review.

Thank you!
Remember, you can get the promised downloads at www.disconnectprinciple.com or scan the QR code.

# APPENDIX: FEEDBACK BEST PRACTICES

---

There is nothing wrong with everything you have been taught about providing feedback.

It's what you *haven't* been taught that is the problem.

There is a missing link that leads you to feeling inadequate, reluctant, anxious, and maybe even mean.

Let's take a quick look at those best practices that I taught Max and that let him down. You may already be familiar with these, so I will review them quickly so everyone knows what I am talking about throughout the book. NOTE: If you have already read this book, the way I describe these best practices should make you grimace. I hope so because this is the typical advice *without* the Disconnect Principle.

The standard advice generally covers five topics. We know these tools and techniques work, but they might not be working for you in the most important situations.

# Five good practices

1. The feedback formula

The feedback formula is an extremely important best practice for feedback, though I am sure there are many variations that use this label. If you are not familiar with this approach, I highly recommend you get familiar with it. But let me cover the basics here very briefly so you know what I am talking about when I refer to the feedback formula.

When giving feedback, it is critical to start with a specific situation in recent memory so the other person knows exactly what moment you are thinking about and neither of you is making generalizations by smooshing multiple blurry, past incidents into one. Here is a good example:

"When we were in the team meeting this morning and I was explaining our new plan,"

The second part of the formula is to focus on a specific, observable behavior because clear facts make for a good starting point free of judgment and assumptions. What exactly did the other person do that you wish to discuss? To continue our example from the meeting, provide a simple fact:

"you contradicted me on the decision that you and I discussed at length just yesterday."

The third part of the formula is to explain why it matters. Discussing impact is often a teachable moment since people often fail to recognize the full impact of their behavior. Specificity, as usual, is important. Adding to the previous example:

> "When you did that, you threw me off topic and made me feel as though our conversation yesterday was for naught. I felt undermined in front of the whole group and we wasted many unnecessary minutes revisiting that decision and getting back on track. It felt like a challenge and made me defensive."

Notice how this expression of impact touched on how the group may have been negatively affected, how the disruption wasted precious time, and how the speaker felt personally. In many cases, lost money, opportunity, and company reputation may also be on the table.

With the situation, observed behavior, and impact laid out on the table as simple, clear facts, the final step is a civil conversation about how to avoid a recurrence or how to deal with the problem created by the incident.

> "Help me understand what you were thinking. If I can understand that, perhaps we can put our heads together and figure out how to prevent this from happening again."

It's an opportunity to hear the other side of the story and learn. The goal is to enter into problem-solving mode and reach mutually agreed conclusions.

The whole point of the feedback formula is to focus on facts, be specific about observed behaviors and the impact of those behaviors, and avoid generalizations and assumptions that cause defensiveness. It's all good stuff.

2. Preparation

I would never discourage preparation. Getting your facts straight is essential to using the feedback formula. Thinking through the impact and being able to state it clearly and in a way the other person can understand is also essential. Taking the time to distinguish between behaviors that really matter and those that may just be annoying, but aren't really of consequence, is part of this preparation as well. In general, you don't want to dive in impulsively, especially if you are angry.

3. Time and Place

I'm sure you've heard that good feedback practices require choosing the time and place wisely.

Privacy is usually critical to an honest discussion. You don't want to express your irritation (Ouch! Disconnect Principle needed!) in a hallway where you can be overheard or at a meeting with others present.

Choosing a time when the other person is able to listen is also important. If they are angry, rushed, or worried about something else, you'll have two or three strikes against you right up front. You also need to avoid being angry, rushed, or worried about something else. But, of course, you don't want to wait too long either. It is best to talk while the incident is fresh in both minds.

4. Format

The advice on format before and after the feedback formula portion of the explanation is more controversial than the previous best practices I've described. Many say to sandwich constructive feedback between positive feedback and encouragement. Others warn that an overly thick sandwich can overpower the meat of the matter and mislead the other person as to how serious the issue really is. Furthermore, for bosses who rarely provide positive feedback on its own, those first words of praise strike fear in the hearts of the recipients because they know the bad news is coming. The initial praise just comes across as insincere. Regardless of which advice you heed, attention to format is important.

5. Carefully Chosen Language

Choosing your words wisely is my last category of best practices. Some of the best advice includes using "I language" and avoiding "Why" questions, but there is much more great advice out there on how to say what you want to say.

# But not good enough

Despite extensive training on how to deliver feedback effectively and how to hold others accountable, we still struggle.

Too often we wimp out and either soften the message so much that the intention is lost or we avoid giving feedback altogether.

Other times, we give it the old college try and limp out feeling miserable and knowing the other person probably feels worse.

But the good news is, many of the tips and techniques we've learned are just great. The something that's been missing is now ready for the taking, and the consequences reach way beyond Max's struggle to give feedback. They will change the way you approach management, accountability, and performance management. Now go back and read the whole book or, if you've read it, appreciate the power of the Disconnect Principle and think about how you would reword this entire Appendix now that you understand what Max didn't.

# THE POWER OF CLARITY BY ANN LATHAM

Don't take it from me! Here is what other readers say about *The Power of Clarity*. (Have you read it? Please leave a review on Amazon.)

The Power of Clarity *will help leaders of every kind sharpen their priorities, improve their process, and find greater meaning in their work.*

Daniel H. Pink, author of *When, Drive,* and *To Sell Is Human*

*Every professional recognizes the importance of clarity – yet it's often hard to come by in the corporate world. With this smart new framework, Ann Latham shows us how to enhance our own clarity, improve team productivity, and create better organizational performance.*

Dorie Clark, Executive Education Professor, Duke University Fuqua School of Business, author of *Reinventing You*

*A critical book for every leader! Learn to give your teams, employees and peers, the clear communication they need to be their most effective and productive in* The Power of Clarity.

Marshall Goldsmith, *NY Times* #1 bestselling author of
*Triggers* and *Mojo*

*If you want to cut through the clutter and chaos of your crazy-busy life, get* The Power of Clarity. *It's filled with rock-solid strategies to help you get the right things done expeditiously.*

Jill Konrath, bestselling author of *More Sales Less Time*
& international speaker

*Ann Latham's book,* The Power of Clarity, *is hands down the best business book I have read in years.*

Joanne Irving, Ph.D., author of *The C$^2$ Factor for Leadership*

*Ann Latham has made the ethereal practical in* The Power of Clarity. *Rich in examples and practical applications, it is a worthy contribution to the science and art of leadership.*

Matt Church, founder Thought Leaders, author of
*Rise Up: An evolution in leadership*

The Power of Clarity *offers profound wisdom and pragmatic tools – industrial strength thinking tools really – for avoiding the activity trap where a bias for action can lead to wasted effort misinterpreted as true progress.*

Chip R. Bell, author of *Inside Your Customer's Imagination*

*Ann Latham is one of the clearest thinkers I know. Her words leap off the page, with an urgency and a call to action that is hard to ignore.*

Jennifer Geary, COO, Asto UK

*As if a book about clarity wouldn't be enough, Ann Latham beautifully lays out a strategy to achieve clarity on all fronts such that it has the power to change how the world works, communicates, and produces. Extremely well done!*

Jeffrey Shaw, author of *The Self-Employed Life* and *LINGO*

*I'm over 100 pages into Ann Latham's book,* The Power of Clarity, *and I'm blown away by the nuggets of wisdom that pop out of every single page.*

Eric Clark, teacher

*This is by far, one of the best business books I've read and I'm recommending it to all my clients.*

Roberta Matuson, author of
*Suddenly In Charge* and *Can We Talk?*

*If you read one business/improvement book this year, make* The Power of Clarity *the one.*

Erica Schoder, Executive Director, RStreet

*We all emphasize the importance of 'clarity,' but that doesn't mean we understand it or practice it. Ann Latham's* The Power of Clarity *is a distillation of what Latham has learned working in over 40 industries with dozens of organizations and leaders (including me).*

John Bidwell, Executive Director,
United Way of Hampshire County

*This is really a big, breakthrough idea. Why do we expect (and get!) precision operation in production processes and tolerate chaotic strategy discussions, messy organizational engagement, revisited decisions, and soul-crushingly endless meetings? Ann Latham has figured it out! And what's better she has offered a way out. Once you read this, it will seem so simple.*

Jane Lansing, Brand Officer and Vice President Marketing,
Emerson Automation Solutions

*Unbelievably packed with insight.*

Dan Neitz, business owner

The Power of Clarity *is a gold mine with nuggets everywhere you look.*

Perry Walraven, CEO, PCI, Inc.

## AVAILABLE IN BOOKSTORES EVERYWHERE INCLUDING AMAZON

# WHO IS ANN LATHAM?

©BLM Photography 2021

I've been dubbed the *Queen of Clarity* by colleagues worldwide such as Steven Robbins, co-designer of Harvard Business School's "Foundations" program, who said, "She's better than anyone I know at finding those places where lack of clarity is getting in the way of progress, and she designs and teaches actionable ways through the ambiguity."

While I fell into this vein of work quite naturally, I didn't recognize my strength until I prepared to start my own consulting business by asking colleagues and bosses, "What is it I do exceptionally well that is most uncommon?" Their wonderful and thoughtful responses established my value proposition and the name of my consulting firm: Uncommon Clarity®.

I left my corporate job with a smile on my face and the only framed award I ever cherished: *Most Likely To Dispute Recognized Authorities.*

I knew I had struck pay dirt several months later when someone introduced me at a networking event by adding, "and she really is uncommonly clear!"

When I tell people my company is Uncommon Clarity, they inevitably reply, "We could use some of that!" But you know what? As much as they like the idea of clarity, they don't know whether they are clear, nor whether it matters. So, while I helped clients ranging from Boeing and Hitachi to Public Broadcasting and United Way with strategic planning, process improvement, and team effectiveness for almost twenty years, I wrote hundreds of articles about clarity. Some of that advice has appeared in *The New York Times*, *Bloomberg*, and *Management Today*. I am also an expert blogger for Forbes.com.

In 2021, I compiled my best thinking into my legacy book, *The Power of Clarity*, which UK management expert Andy Bass said, "does for knowledge workers what *Lean Thinking* and *The Toyota Way* did for the factory floor!" I am also the author of *The Clarity Papers* and *Uncommon Meetings*, and now, *The Disconnect Principle*, a topic I care about deeply, but which just wouldn't fit in *The Power of Clarity*.

Contact me at: AnnLatham.com

# MORE PRAISE FOR THE DISCONNECT PRINCIPLE

*I wish I had read this great book when I was a manager...or the parent of a teenager! I honestly thought I knew a lot about feedback, performance management, and accountability; until I read* The Disconnect Principle. *It is profound, fresh and filled with practical wisdom.*

Chip R. Bell, author of *Inside Your Customer's Imagination*

*Despite all the books, training and coaching on giving feedback and having tough performance management conversations, managers still struggle. Ann Latham has the missing link. You only need to buy one more book: this one.*

Andy Bass, PhD, author of *Start With What Works* and *Committed Action*

The Disconnect Principle *could change the way you approach feedback, both giving and receiving, forever! Running a small, remote team means I'm frequently giving and receiving feedback, holding people accountable and being held accountable. It's a situation rife for miscommunication, confusion and finger-pointing! After reading* The Disconnect Principle *I had a new way of thinking about my own (dated!) methodology. I now know how to stay out of the trap of trying to fix the person (which isn't possible) by using her framework to fix the situation. Ann has distilled a complicated topic into an easy-to-read, easy-to-apply book. She makes it possible to take the ideas and examples in her book, apply them immediately in your leadership role and see positive results that make you feel better prepared to lead others.*

Debbie Jenkins, author of *Stop Writing Books Nobody Reads*

*I am only half way through* The Disconnect Principle, *however, I already love it! It makes complete sense to me that approaching feedback by saying we have a disconnect vs. I have some constructive feedback to give you changes everything. I actually used this today without planning on it because someone approached me in an aggressive manner, upset about a perceived issue. It worked like magic and I will definitely use it again.*

Stacy Meyer, Project Manager, Philips

*Ann Latham provides details and numerous examples on how to provide feedback with empathy and clarity in* The Disconnect Principle. *Every leader should understand the difference between 'doing TO' and 'doing WITH.' I recommend this book to any leader and as one to include in leadership book studies.*

Janet Ply, PhD, author of *Luck Is Not a Strategy*

*In this book Ann Latham is, to use her direct and simple way of putting things, 'identifying a really common occurrence'. It is important just to realise how big a difference it makes to focus on the disconnect between two people rather than on who is right and who is wrong, but I encourage you to read* the whole book carefully to embed the principle. Ann analyses typical situations that illustrate the subtle but incredibly powerful differences it makes to work from the starting point of The Disconnect Principle and then to work with someone rather than doing things to them, however difficult the situation is. I am very pleased to have discovered The Disconnect Principle, and Ann's other book, The Power of Clarity, is next on my list!

Judy Barber, coach, facilitator, speaker, and author of
*The Slow Coach Approach*

We all make assumptions to get through the day; so too do all those with whom we interact. Some of those turn out to be true, but many do not. As we seek to build mutual trust and respect, those assumptions can interfere. In The Disconnect Principle Ann Latham gives us tools to eliminate building those assumptions into our conversations, getting us where we want to be without creating needless friction. Her examples are helpful, reflecting situations we all face. A quick read supported by internalizing the tools can help anyone succeed in building a healthy culture.

Rebecca Morgan, president, Fulcrum ConsultingWorks Inc

It's such a simple but important concept outlined with the uncommon clarity I've come to know and love from author Ann Latham. While I think it should be required reading for all managers, it should definitely be required reading for managers who hate conflict. With this book and the principles it teaches, there doesn't need to be conflict! The book is well organized for easy reading and filled with very specific *applicable concepts that can be put into action immediately. The book even offers language you can use for different scenarios until you get into your own comfort zone with deploying the Disconnect Principle. Within the first day of reading the book (it's a short read by the way), I used the Disconnect Principle twice – once with an employee and once at a meeting of our Senior Leadership team. I didn't even break a sweat and even better, in both circumstances it opened up the dialogue for meaningful conversation and progress.*

Kristin Cole, Vice President of Workforce Development,
Greenfield Community College

*My coaching clients often unintentionally introduce friction when providing feedback that is meant to enhance performance. The Disconnect Principle provides a framework and language to help us avoid the risk of making things worse rather than better in feedback situations like these.*

Gena Cox, PhD, organizational psychologist,
author of *Leading Inclusion*

*'We have a disconnect.' This will now be my new go-to phrase when something isn't going the way I'm expecting. It so swiftly diffuses a situation to get at the circumstances and not at the people involved. Cut through the drama! That's what starting with this phrase will do. Lower everyone's armor and start working more quickly toward clarity (yes, from Ann's previous book* The Power of Clarity*). The Disconnect Principle is a powerful practice in both professional and personal situations.*

*And, as you'd expect from Ann, it's simple to follow and start practicing immediately.*

*Adrienne Guerrerro, founder, Positive Delta, LLC*

*Good feedback is crucial to learning. Learning is crucial to making change happen. Anyone who is leading a team through change should read* The Disconnect Principle. *Consistently apply the simple yet profound principles Ann describes and demonstrates in this book and you will avoid a tremendous amount of stress, alleviate much unnecessary productivity loss and improve the quality of worklife for you and your team as you navigate change in your workplace.*

Dr. Louise A. Harris, Founder, Change Design Institute

*With uncommon clarity, Ann Latham shares fresh strategies to deal with challenging people and performance issues. Not only are they easy to implement, but they're also highly effective.*

Jill Konrath, author of *SNAP Selling, More Sales Less Time* and *Selling to Big Companies*

*With her trademark precision, Latham dissects the difficult conversations we have every day and proposes a better way.* The Disconnect Principle *re-wires those conversations, and shows how to inject empathy and sincerity into your interactions.*

Jennifer Geary, author of *How to be a Chief Risk Officer*

*I work in an industry with many highly intelligent and motivated experts. They are generally distrustful of any systems or frameworks they haven't taken part in creating. Working on the Disconnect Principle with my teams started from a place I would generously characterize as apathetic. But the truest testament of how we've come to value the framework is hearing my colleagues say "I think we have a disconnect" or questioning, "How can we approach this in a way that does With and not To?"*

Chad Russell, Associate Vice President, R Street Institute

*I desperately want my leadership to not just read this book, but to commit it to memory and then have us* both *PRACTICE the tips and guidance it amply provides (e.g., WITH versus TO).*

Andy O'Hearn, Associate Director, Communication & Change Management, Bayer Pharmaceuticals

Made in the USA
Monee, IL
28 December 2022

23976764R00085